# Smart Business for Contractors

## A Guide to Money and the Law

JIM KRAMON

The Taunton Press

**Publisher:** Jim Childs

**Acquisitions Editor:** Steve Culpepper

**Editors:** Jacquelyn Callahan Parente, Peter Chapman

**Copy Editor:** Diane Sinitsky

**Indexer:** Lynda Stannard

**Cover Designer:** Steve Hughes

**Interior Design:** Ecomlinks, Inc.

**Layout:** Ecomlinks, Inc., and Lynne Phillips

**Cover Photographer:** Scott Phillips

Taunton
BOOKS & VIDEOS
*for fellow enthusiasts*

The Taunton Press, Inc., 63 South Main Street, PO Box 5506,
Newtown, CT 06470-5506
e-mail: tp@taunton.com

For Pros/By Pros® is a trademark of The Taunton Press, Inc., registered in
the U.S. Patent and Trademark Office.

Distributed by Publishers Group West

**Library of Congress Cataloging-in-Publication Data:**

Kramon, Jim.

For Pros/By Pros®: Smart business for contractors : a guide to money and the
law / Jim Kramon.

p. cm.

Includes index.

ISBN 1-56158-411-8

1. Construction industry--United States--Management. 2. Building trades--
United States--Management. 3. Construction industry--United States--Personnel
management. 4. Building trades--United States--Personnel management. 5. Labor laws
and legislation--United States. 6. Construction industry--Law and legislation--United
States. 7. Contractors--Legal status, laws, etc.--United States. I. Title.

**NOTE:** *The Taunton Press does not intend the material presented in* Smart
Business for Contractors *to function as a substitute for professional legal, tax, and
accounting advice. In matters that involve local, state, or federal regulations, contractors
should seek additional advice from government agencies and an attorney. Information
on taxes and accounting is based on the tax code as of 2000. Check with the IRS or
an accountant for current tax requirements.*

# ◼Acknowledgments

Many people have helped me bring this book to fruition. Let me name just a few. Valerie Lazzaro of American Express Small Business Services was helpful in verifying tax matters and providing information regarding tax forms and filings. Jill Glassman of Glassman Pension Services provided important information with regard to qualified retirement plans. As she has on so many occasions, Sandra Cooley of Sandra K. Cooley & Associates generously gave her time to review medical insurance matters with me. I have never known anyone more knowledgeable about this subject than Sandra.

I am indebted to contractors too numerous to mention for their time and information. Through these discussions I have been able to learn what contractors know and do not know and what their needs and desires are. Since it is for their benefit that this book is written, these discussions were invaluable.

My friend and general contractor, Phil Florie, assisted in this book in many ways. I deeply appreciate the many hours he spent helping me. Steve Culpepper at The Taunton Press is responsible for making the engagement with me to write this book. Steve's appreciation of this subject and his consideration and forthrightness made the whole process easy and enjoyable. The experience and steadiness of my editor at Taunton, Peter Chapman, kept me on more than one occasion from straying from the job I had set out to do. It has been a pleasure working for someone as capable and considerate as Peter.

My editor, Jackie Parente of Editorial Services, LLC, is what every writer of a book hopes to experience. Jackie's knowledge and understanding of the subject matter, her uncompromised attention to detail, and her ability to explain what is readable and what is not made this a much better book.

I could not have completed this book without the help of Nancy Sumwalt, a paralegal in my law firm with whom I have had the privilege of working for almost 15 years. Nancy organized and prepared every chapter of this book. She verified countless facts and assertions and was my constant liaison with my editors. Nancy also reviewed the entire manuscript. Most important, Nancy has always been able to tell me, in her quiet and definite way, when I have plainly missed the mark. I am very grateful for Nancy's hard work.

While I am indebted to these people for their invaluable assistance in writing this book, I am solely responsible for all content.

# Contents

# Introduction

**E**ver since I was a child, I have admired the work of contractors. In the small apartment building where I grew up, I would follow the building's superintendent—a plumber, electrician, carpenter, and everything else—whenever he came to fix whatever was broken or, for a few dollars from my mother, add a shelf or install a new appliance. When he would leave, I would use household utensils, brooms, and mops to imitate his tools so that I could pretend to be doing what he did. Sometimes on weekends, my mother would take me to a nearby lumberyard where the workmen gave me leftover scraps of 2x4s and plywood, which I would take home to make into crude toys and furniture.

In later years, I worked for builders while in school and got a closer look at their lifestyles. From scattered conversations throughout the day, I came to realize the hardship and precariousness of the lives of most contractors. The very same man whose tilework or woodwork or roofing or flooring was so carefully and seamlessly completed was often unable to pay his mortgage, get proper medical care for his family, or make reasonable plans to retire someday.

Since that time, I have practiced law for 30 years and represented quite a few contractors. I have also had many opportunities to deal with owners, architects, engineers, and others involved in construction projects in matters ranging from the smallest engagements of contractors by private owners to large development projects involving general contractors or construction managers. What struck me as I learned about the lives of contractors is the contrast that often exists between the skill and integrity of a contractor's work and the frequently haphazard manner in which his business and financial affairs are organized.

I know contractors who don't have liability or medical insurance. I know contractors who have no plan whatsoever for retirement or disability. Very few of the contractors I have discussed the matter with get all of the tax benefits available to them. It is an unusual contractor who is aware of his choices about retirement plans.

Contractors are not alone in these shortcomings, but it is disturbing to see people with highly developed skills in their crafts who lack the business skills that deeply affect their lifestyles. In these activities, I have found that my sympathies lie with the men and women who perform the actual work, the contractors themselves, and it is this feeling that has been the primary motivation for this book.

In one respect, the work life of a contractor is the same as every service provider. Anyone who makes his living providing services has nothing to sell unless he gets up in the morning and does whatever it is that provides his service. But in other respects, contractors are different from other service providers. Usually, if they don't do it, it doesn't get done. The buck stops right where it starts. You can save the word "delegate" for bigger businesses.

The independence that attracts many contractors to their work often brings with it difficulties. The self-reliant nature of contractors haunts them in many ways that affect their financial securities. The majority of contractors work alone or in small groups that don't operate like other established businesses.

What is a minor glitch for workers in many types of work is a showstopper for a contractor. A broken truck for a contractor doesn't simply mean finding an alternative way to get to work. It means, more often than not, that the contractor can't do his work and earn his income. A pricing mistake for a dentist means at worst a short-term loss on one small part of his business. For a contractor, however, a faulty takeoff from plans for a job that will last six or eight weeks may mean bankruptcy. Similarly, bad knees for a contractor who does flooring or carpet installation or neck pain for one who does ceilings or overhead lighting will probably mean disability sooner or later.

In the year or so before I started to write this book, I asked contractors some very direct questions: "Do you use an accountant? What sort of retirement plan do you have? Why did you decide to use a corporation and is it helpful to you? If I wrote a book to provide you with all the information you would like to have, what would you like to see in it?" From the answers to these questions, I have learned what contractors generally know and don't know and, most important, what they would like to know. I hope that I have also learned the best ways to explain to contractors matters that may not be particularly exciting for them.

This book is my best effort to include in one manageable volume everything the typical contractor needs to know about business matters. I have tried to provide specific and useful information wherever possible; when that is not possible, I have directed you to the best and most convenient sources of information. I have outlined each business topic with simple, easy-to-follow, and time-saving steps. I am well aware that the finished product of learning and following good business practices is not like the finished jobs most contractors try to do. If you learn the information that is in this book and follow the recommended steps, your reward will not be a beautifully pointed-up brick wall or perfectly fitted custom cabinets. But it will be more money and more financial security for you and your family as a result of the hard work you are doing.

As I think about contractors following the advice that I offer in this book, I think about the work of my friend Phil Florie. I have been fortunate to enjoy Phil's exceptional skills in a number of renovations to my home. Phil's approach to each project is planned and performed with precision, dedication, and skill. It's a real joy to watch Phil execute his trade and enjoy the results. The outcome is always beautiful, functional, and cost-effective. I doubt if many readers of this book will find the steps that I describe in this book as interesting as I have found watching the progress of these many projects. It is my hope, nevertheless, that your next project—to create for yourself the most lucrative and financially secure life your work can make possible—will work out as well as Phil's projects. If you follow each of the steps carefully, it will.

# CHAPTER 1

# Money Matters:
## Pricing, Billing, Collecting

**Y**ou are a contractor. You know your trade, you're good at it, and most days you enjoy what you're doing. These are some of the reasons that you're in business. But another important reason is to make money. This chapter will help you learn how to convert your hard work into a profitable business that gives financial security to you and your family. There are three key areas that I'll cover:

- **PRICING JOBS:** You'll learn to charge an hourly rate that will allow you to price each job accurately while considering both your financial goals and the expenses involved. Using this method will help you to stay profitable without getting overwhelmed by paperwork.

- **INCLUDING EXPENSES IN YOUR COSTS:** Expenses are part of your cost of doing business and they can be valuable tax deductions, so you don't want to overlook any of them. I'll cover which expenses are just part of running your business, or overhead, and which expenses you can bill directly to your customer. In chapter 4, I'll go into detail about tracking and organizing these expenses—without pain.

- **BILLING AND COLLECTING:** You'll learn how to avoid common billing problems, keep your billing simple yet as professional as your work, and get paid quickly.

# How to Price Your Work

As a contractor, you are a service provider. Rather than selling a product that you can touch or hold, like a hammer, you are selling your time. Everyone who provides a service gets paid for only one thing—the amount of time it takes to do the work. While you also charge for the materials that you use to do the job, such as lumber or tile, your greatest value lies in the skills you have learned in your trade. Just like accountants, lawyers, or computer technicians, you need to decide how much those skills are worth and convert that to an hourly rate for your services.

Some contractors avoid the hourly rate approach and simply say, "I'll charge as much as I can for each job and this will give me as much profit as possible." This sounds good, but it doesn't work. Why not? There are two main reasons:

1. If you don't look at the time involved, it's tempting to accept jobs where the highest possible price is still too low to make it worth your time *(profitable)*.

2. If you don't consider what you are charging per hour, you can't compare jobs on the basis of profitability (how much will you really earn rather than how large is your bill). The job that seems to pay the most money doesn't necessarily earn you the most money when you consider how much you earn per hour.

As the example below shows, the contractor who builds the deck earns $50 per hour as opposed to the builder who lays a plank floor and earns only $28 per hour. It's not surprising that if you speak with contractors in various trades, you'll discover that those who price their work on an hourly rate basis have the highest annual incomes. They don't take unprofitable jobs, and they choose between jobs in a way that provides them with the best ones in terms of profit.

Pricing your job involves four basic steps:

1. Determine an hourly rate using the hourly rate approach described below.

2. Estimate the number of hours that a particular job will take.

3. Multiply the number of hours by the hourly rate.

4. Add the cost of materials and other expenses involved with that job.

**Q: Can I lower my prices when work is slow?**

**A:** That's a tough question with an even tougher answer. It's surely tempting to reduce prices when you're getting started or when work is scarce. If at all possible, don't do it. Hold your prices at their fair value.

It's easy to get the reputation as a low-ball hitter, and once you lower your rates, it's pretty tough to raise them after the crisis is over. A contractor who sets a fair hourly rate and consistently prices does better in the long run than one who lowers his prices to meet short-term needs. It's not easy, but hang tough.

## Using the Hourly Rate Approach

To use the hourly rate approach to pricing your work, consider these things:

- How much do you want to earn per year?

- How many hours do you want to spend each year doing your work?

- What are your expenses in running your business *(general overhead)?*

- How much time will a particular job take?

- What expenses should be charged to that job *(variable expenses)?*

The next section explains why it's important to set income goals first and how to set them. I'll cover how to figure reasonably the number of hours that you'll work and how many of those you can plan to get paid for; which expenses you should include in your hourly rate; and how to estimate the time and expenses for a particular job so that you can profitably quote it.

*A good estimate is that 70% of the workday is actual work time.*

## ■ Setting your income

It may seem strange to set your income goal first, but the point of this book is to put you in control of your business. Set your intended income reasonably, but set it. If you have any questions about what is a fair and reasonable income for your profession, there are various sources that can help. If you get trade magazines for your profession, look at the ads to see what other contractors are charging.

Perhaps the best place to obtain information about pricing in your trade is to speak with other contractors. You can probably tell which contractors are making more money than others, and you should speak with the ones who seem to be most successful. On those occasions when you learn of the bids by other contractors for jobs you are bidding on, you can figure out the approximate hourly rates the others are charging for their time by working backward. Remember, however, that it is unlawful to agree upon (fix) prices.

## ■ Estimating your actual work time

The next step for figuring the correct hourly rate for your work is to estimate as precisely as possible how much time you will spend working for a full year. This sounds like a big job, but it's easier than you think. There are two approaches that you can use. Pick the one that's easiest for you.

1. Review a typical three-month period of your work schedule and use that as the basis for a yearly estimate. To do this:

   ■ Check your financial records, calendar, and any other records you have to identify every job you did during that three-month period.

---

**TIP**

**ESTIMATING TIME**

- Keep a log of the time that you spend on jobs. This will help with future estimates.
- Talk with fellow contractors to see how long certain projects take them.
- How long did it take to do a similar job? Use that as a starting point.
- Things typically take longer than you expect, so build that into your estimate.
- Balance a reasonable number of hours with a competitive price, but never underestimate hours just to get the job.

- Make a note of each job listed in your calendar, checkbook, and so on, and estimate approximately how much time you spent on each job.

- Add up the hours for the three-month period and multiply by four to provide a good estimate of the number of hours you can expect to work in a full year.

> **Q:** **Why is the hourly rate method of pricing best?**
> **A:** 
> - You make the most money.
> - It helps you avoid unprofitable jobs.
> - It makes sure that all of your expenses are fairly passed on to your customer.
> - It helps you to determine your annual income.
> - It makes clear the financial impact of working different amounts of time.
> - It helps you distinguish between expenses that are part of your general overhead and expenses that are part of a particular job.
> - Your pricing is clear, fair, and reasonable, and you can defend your prices to anyone.

2. Estimate the number of hours per week you work for which you get paid *(billable hours)*. The important words here are "work for which you get paid." You need to look at the time that you "work" and then take away time that you don't get paid for. Start with your usual workday—let's call it 10 hours.

- Take out the time driving to and from your jobs and to and from your suppliers.

- Take out lunch and breaks.

- Take out time spent preparing estimates, talking with prospective customers, banking, talking to your accountant, and so on.

- Take out any other time that is not for work performed.

A good estimate is that 70% of the workday is actual work time. That means that if you work a 50-hour week most of the time, your actual work time averages around 35 hours per week.

Whichever approach they use to estimate their time, very few contractors find that they spend more than 2,000 hours per year performing their work. Although most contractors are on their job sites more time than this, their actual work time (the time that they can charge for) is substantially less.

> **Q:** **How many hours can I expect to work in a year?**
> **A:** A good rule of thumb is 1,500 hours per year of work that you can charge for. This may turn out to be a little low, but it's a good starting place.

## ■ Estimating general overhead expenses

After you have set your goals for annual income and number of hours of actual work, the next step is to total your general overhead expenses and add that number to the income you intend to earn.

General overhead expenses are expenses involved in running your business that aren't related to any particular job. They are also called *fixed expenses*. For example, the cost of maintaining your pickup truck, tools, fax machine, insurance, matching Social Security and Medicare payments, phone, and other such costs are fixed expenses. The other type of expense, known as *variable expenses*, is tied directly to a particular job. The most obvious variable expense is the cost of the materials for a job, such as lumber, tile, and circuit breakers (see pp. 13–14 for more on variable expenses).

Here's a simple way to estimate your general overhead expenses. Look at the "General Overhead Expenses" checklist on the facing page for a summary of fixed expense items. Using this checklist as a starting point, do the following:

1. Review your checkbook and business receipts for one full year to find all general overhead expenses (see chapter 4 for ways to easily organize your expense records).

---

### General Overhead vs. Variable Expenses

**General overhead expenses** are costs involved in running your business as a whole and are not associated with just one job. Rent, insurance, office equipment, and vehicles are good examples.

**Variable expenses** apply to just one job. The materials that you use are part of the cost of doing a job, even if you have them in your inventory and do not purchase them especially for a particular job. Variable expenses may also include labor of employees, special insurance, waste removal, fees for permits, and numerous other items.

In you're not sure, ask yourself, "Would I buy this if I weren't doing this job?" If the answer is "no," then this is probably a variable expense.

2. Make a list showing each expense item and the cost.

3. Total all items. This is your general overhead for one year. (If you have been in business for less than a year—six months, for example—multiply this by two.)

General overhead expenses are paid as surely as bills for supplies for particular jobs. A plumber would certainly not install a new sink and toilet without including them in his bill. The contractor who does not take into account the expenses of running his entire business when pricing his work is cheating himself just as much as one who does not take material costs into account.

**TIP**

**REMEMBER YOUR GENERAL OVERHEAD**
Don't forget to include your general overhead in your hourly rate. If you leave out expenses that you pay to run your business, you will lower your annual income substantially.

### General Overhead Expenses

- Insurance expenses related to the business
  - Vehicle insurance
  - General liability insurance
  - Workers' compensation and unemployment insurance, where applicable
  - Other insurance
- Expenses of pickup trucks or other vehicles
  - Maintenance and repairs
  - Gas and oil
  - Annual allotment for replacement cost (this is based upon the price of the vehicle, the trade-in value of the vehicle when it is used up, and the number of years in the vehicle's life for the contractor)
  - Cellular telephone costs
- Office overhead (fax, phone, computer, stationery, pens and pencils)
- Expenses of tools
- Expenses of maintaining machinery
- Magazines, dues for trade associations
- Accountant's and lawyer's fees

Note: See the Internal Revenue Service or your accountant regarding tax questions. This list is not meant to be a tax guide.

## ■ Computing your hourly rate

Now that you have set your estimated annual income, the hours you plan to work each year, and your general overhead expenses, computing your hourly rate is simple math:

1. Add the annual total for general overhead to your expected annual income.

2. Divide the sum of general overhead and expected annual income by the total number of hours you expect to work. The result is the hourly rate to charge for every job.

Let's look at an example. Joe is a roofer who wants to make his business more profitable. He knows that he should be able to make $50,000 a year from his roofing business. He is able to work about 1,600 billable hours a year and has general overhead for one year of $14,000.

Here's the math:

$50,000 (income) + $14,000 (overhead) = $64,000
$64,000 ÷ 1,600 hours = $40 per hour

To make the income that he deserves, Joe needs to charge $40 per hour.

## ■ Estimating time per job

Now that you know how much to charge per hour, you need to estimate how much time each job will take. As mentioned earlier, some contractors don't think in terms of hours when they are pricing jobs. This is a mistake because you risk working many hours for which you don't charge and thus don't get paid.

Estimating your time can be a challenge if you haven't been in your trade for very long. However, if you've been in business for a while, you have a pretty good feel for how long it takes to build a deck or lay a kitchen floor. In either case, your own experience, sometimes assisted by discussions with others, will generally provide a good basis for estimat-

**TIP**

**GENERAL OVERHEAD TAX DEDUCTIBILITY**
While you need to know about your general overhead expenses when you file your taxes, don't confuse pricing your work with filing your taxes. Always check with the IRS or your accountant if you have questions about what's deductible on your taxes.

> **Time and Materials Billing**
>
> Time and materials (T & M) billing is based on the customer trusting you to tell him how much time you are spending on the job and how much money you are paying for supplies and other costs of the work. You then charge the customer accordingly. The customer and contractor must agree upon the contractor's hourly rate, and the contractor must keep an honest record of his work time. T & M billing is good for the contractor because it takes away the guesswork of estimates. Unfortunately, most jobs are not priced on a time and materials basis.

ing the time it will take to do a particular job. This isn't the same thing as charging for time and materials (T & M). Although T & M is by far the better pricing method, contractors rarely have an opportunity to use it (see the sidebar above).

When you arrive at what you think is a good, reasonable time estimate, add another 5% to 10% to it. That's not to line your pockets—it's to protect your wallet. The saying about "expect the unexpected" holds very true here; there will almost always be a complication or delay that you haven't foreseen. Once you have signed a contract it's difficult, if not impossible, to revise the quote.

## ■ Tracking variable expenses

The final step in pricing a job is to include the price of all materials and all special costs related to a job. These costs can be easy to overlook, but forgetting them destroys the profit of a job. Variable expenses fall into several categories:

- **MATERIALS:** These are the building materials that you use just for that job. This includes lumber, nails, tile, roofing, switches, and so on. Even if you keep an inventory of these items, such as the lumber or the nails, you need to break out how much of your inventory you used for this job and charge the current price for them (not the price you may have paid a year ago). Do not use the price of materials from a previous job, since material prices may change unexpectedly.

- **REMOVAL OF MATERIALS:** Some jobs require the removal of soil, brush, debris, or other materials. Many areas require the disposal of such materials at special sites, often with a dumping fee. This is true for trash generally and especially for materials that are classified as hazardous. Include all costs related to the removal of materials in the pricing of a job.

- **PERMITS:**  Include the costs of any special permits needed for a particular job.

- **LABOR:**  You've already figured your own labor costs in the job using the hourly rate. Don't forget to charge if you're going to use additional labor on a job. Whether you are using your own employee, a subcontractor, or simply temporary laborers or assistants, include those labor costs in the job. Remember, however, if you are using your own employees, the matching contributions for Social Security and Medicare (FICA), workers' compensation, and unemployment insurance are part of your general overhead expenses.

- **ALLOWANCES:**  Sometimes there are expenses related to a job that are impossible to estimate exactly. This can happen if the architect gives a general description of an item to be used rather than a specific model number or if the customer wishes to upgrade an item to a better-quality one. Some of the other costs that were listed previously, such as waste disposal and additional labor, can't be estimated exactly. When you don't know what the exact amount will be, the best way to protect yourself is to include an allowance in your price. With an allowance, you tell the customer what you expect the cost to be, but you also include a statement that if the cost goes up, so will the price. Building contractors routinely use allowances for items such as carpeting. The estimate includes a reasonable amount for the carpet, but if the owner wants something more expensive, he will need to pay the additional cost.

Every expense of a contractor must be accounted for either as general overhead or as a cost related to a particular job. Contractors who pay costs that are not taken into account one way or another destroy their profitability. Chapter 4 gives you easy-to-use ways to keep these expenses organized.

## ■ Putting it all together—the quote

The final step in pricing your work is to combine all of these items into a quote for your customer. Don't do this step casually; you'll really be cheating yourself if you do. And pick a time when you are free from distractions, such as after dinner or Sunday afternoon. It's well worth the investment. Contractors who prepare their quotes carefully are far more profitable than those who don't. You don't get a second chance with a careless estimate, and there's no way to make a poorly priced job profitable.

Use the "Checklist for Pricing Your Work" as a step-by-step guide for pricing jobs correctly. With it, you're sure to include all the essential elements of a profitable price.

*You don't get a second chance with a careless estimate, and there's no way to make a poorly priced job profitable.*

---

**Checklist for Pricing Your Work**

1. Set the hourly rate for your work based upon the number of hours you plan to work each year, the income you plan to earn, and the cost of your general overhead.
2. Estimate the number of hours the job will take, allowing a little room for errors and oversights. Past experience and talking with others may be helpful.
3. Multiply the numbers from steps 1 and 2 to figure how much to charge for your time. If the owner is willing to pay you on a time and materials basis, you can skip this step.
4. Add up the expenses related to that job (not general overhead expenses).
   - Be sure to include all special costs such as waste disposal, special insurance, employees, other contractors, and so forth.
   - Be sure to include all costs of materials at verified prices, including replacement cost of items taken from your inventory.
   - Include allowances for those costs that may change.
5. Be sure that every cost is accounted for—either as a general overhead item or as a cost item related to the particular job.
6. Add the numbers from steps 3 and 4 to come up with your job price.
7. If there are parts of the price that you feel may change, increase your price to protect yourself. Remember, it's very hard to increase a price once you have agreed to it.

To see how this works, let's go back to our roofer, Joe. We already know that he needs to charge $40 per hour to cover his income and fixed expenses. Joe is bidding on a job to put a new shingle roof on a house. He will need to repair some of the sheathing, replace the flashing and gutters, and lay down two thicknesses of roofing paper. It should take him not quite three eight-hour days to do the work. The shingles, nails, sheathing, roofing paper, flashing, gutter parts, and miscellaneous small items will cost a little less than $2,650. (He's added a little extra to cover unforeseen expenses.) Here's how Joe prices the job:

> Job will take 24 hours
> 24 hours x $40 per hour = $960
> Expenses = $2,650
> $960 + $2,650 = $3,610

This brings the total price for the job to $3,610. To protect his income, Joe should not offer to do the job at less than this price. If possible, Joe may charge a higher price, which he then knows will fully protect his income and his need to account for all of his expenses.

## Keeping Track of Expenses

Keeping track of expenses is vital both to establishing your hourly rate and to making sure that you pass along to your customer all the expenses involved in the project. There may also be tax benefits, but I'll go into that in chapter 7. When you are ready to prepare the bill for your customer, you need to have a list of the materials and supplies that you used and the costs involved. It's almost impossible to remember at billing time every expense that you paid for a job. Keeping track of expenses may seem like a simple thing, but if you don't do it right, you're throwing money away.

Even when a job is priced at a fixed price for all work and materials, it's important to know what expenses were actually paid for the job so that you'll know for future purposes whether the job was profitable. If the hourly rate method is correctly used to price a job and all necessary materials and other expenses are anticipated and properly billed, the job should be a profitable one.

# Billing and Collecting Payments for Your Work

You priced the job well, kept track of all the expenses, did a beautiful job, and the customer is happy. There's one final—and very important—task left: getting paid. Some contractors start to lose interest when paperwork is mentioned, but stick with it. Billing and collecting can be almost painless. And without it, you won't get paid. When done the right way, your bills will get paid sooner, with fewer disagreements, and the number of bills that go uncollected will dwindle. There are six important steps to remember in billing:

1. Get a down payment whenever possible—and it's almost always possible (subject to state law).

2. As soon as the job is done, send a neat, professional bill to the customer.

3. If the job is a long one, send regular bills during the course of the work.

4. Follow up immediately with a "friendly reminder" if your customer does not pay within the agreed-upon amount of time.

5. If the job is ongoing, stop work and send your customer a "final demand."

6. If the "final demand" doesn't work, send the bill to a collections agency.

## ■ Avoiding high-risk customers

First rule for successful billing: Don't work for people who aren't likely to pay. You might ask, "How do I know if a customer is a bad risk?" The simple answer is that you can't always know, but there are certain warning signs that can tip you off. Look for these clues:

- **A BAD PAYMENT RECORD:** People who do not respect the value of work of others at one time tend not to do so in the future. When you know that someone has failed to pay contractors in the past, it's best either not to work for that person or to insist upon payment in advance.

**TIP**

**CHECK YOUR STATE'S RULES ON DOWN PAYMENTS**
Some states do not permit you to require a down payment exceeding a certain amount or percentage of total job cost. Most states have a publicly available office to answer questions about state law dealing with consumer protection issues. This office is frequently within the Office of the State Attorney General.

*First rule for successful billing: Don't work for people who aren't likely to pay.*

- **SPECULATIVE TO THE POINT OF RECKLESSNESS:** The owner who has never had a successful restaurant but now intends to spend hundreds of thousands of dollars renovating and furnishing a new 75-seat restaurant is a classic example of recklessness. Most such ventures fail, and when they do, local newspapers often identify the parties who got "stiffed," most of these being contractors.

- **ARGUMENTATIVE:** Trust your instincts on this one. If someone finds problems with your plans for doing the job, you can bet he is going to find problems with your bills. If someone disagrees with you about matters that are within your expertise, there's a good chance that person will disagree with you about money. Even if you follow the correct steps for properly making an agreement with a client, the client who simply does not like to pay for services will find difficulties with what you did. In using your instincts, be careful that they don't lead you to discriminate against any customers for any reason other than sound business ones. The law deals harshly with any business that discriminates against any group of people for reasons that don't simply reflect sound business judgment. When someone offers his goods or services to the public, the goods and services must be offered fairly and evenly to anyone who wants them.

Take heart, there are resources to help you determine if a customer is a high risk. Credit information is listed in a number of publicly available places. You must be careful, however, that any place you look for such information is publicly available and that you use whatever information you obtain from such sources in a legal manner. If you're not sure, a short consultation with an attorney can save you a lot of difficulty.

You'll find that there is usually more information publicly available about businesses than about people. If the information available to you isn't sufficient to justify the size job you are considering doing for a customer, don't be shy about asking that person or business for references. If a person or business can't give any references and wants you to do a large job with a great deal of financial risk, you're probably better off turning down the job.

## ■ Asking for payments in advance of work

Ask for a substantial advance payment on all work that you do (subject to state laws). You might want to waive this for customers you know very well or for very small jobs (less than $500), but if you want to make your business more profitable, make advance payment a rule you always follow. You may feel awkward at first and be eager to get into the work before requesting any payment, but advance payments are reasonable and customary business practices. You should have no reluctance about insisting on them. Include the amount of the advance payment in the estimate that you give to your customer. If the owner objects, walk away from the job. If the owner objects to the advance, he will most likely find other objections down the road. Reasonable owners understand reasonable business practices.

Here are some rules of thumb to use in deciding how much the advance should be:

- Depending upon the materials that you have to buy, advances may vary between 10% and 50% of the entire contract price.

- If the job is short, the percentage of payment requested in advance should be greater.

- For those jobs where the cost of materials is substantial, it is reasonable to request an advance of at least the cost of materials.

- Check your state's regulations to make sure that advance payments are allowed.

## ■ Preparing the bill

Whether you collected an advance or not, you will need to send the owner a bill to collect the money due to you. Yes, this falls into the "paperwork" category, so many contractors feel that they just don't have the time to do this or to do it in a professional manner. If you want to be successful and profitable, sending your bills on time—every time—is a task that you don't have the luxury to avoid.

**Rules for successful billing**   Billing doesn't need to be complicated or time-consuming, but there are a few important rules to follow that help ensure that your customers will pay you when they should.

---

■ **John T. Smith**
**REGISTERED ELECTRICIAN**
209 Apple Way
Podunk, Pennsylvania 00000
August 9, 2001

---

**Invoice**
■ **PROGRESS BILLING:**

Wiring all fixtures and appliances in new master bedroom and bath addition to house at 49 Seefield Court, Plymouth, Pennsylvania 00000, including ceiling and other fixtures, outlets, baseboard heater in bathroom, through-the-wall air conditioner in master bedroom.

Work and materials through July 31, 2001
$5,287.51

■ **TERMS:**
Payment due within 30 days.
Thereafter, interest will accrue at the rate of 1½% per month.

**TIP**

Always make it clear if the bill is a progress bill and not a final bill.

1. Make your bills as professional as your work:   Prepare your bills on your company stationery—not on scraps of paper. They should be typed (or done on a computer) and should explain their purpose. You can get blank billing forms (called invoices) at an office-supply store. If you have a computer, you can make an invoice using a word-processing program or you can even buy very economical billing software (see pp. 48–49 for a discussion on computers and whether you need one). A professional-looking bill demands payment far more than a sloppy bill.

2. Send bills on time—every time:   Send the bill to the customer promptly—not more than one week after finishing the job (see the next rule for jobs lasting more than a month). Gratitude for work all but vanishes within a week or two. It's very important that the bill for the work be in the owner's hands before the gratitude ends.

■ **Mark Q. Schroeder**
**CUSTOM CARPENTRY**
1124 Woodlawn Drive
Oakley, Pennsylvania 00000
August 9, 2001

## Invoice
■ **FINAL BILLING:**

Installation of new door and shelving in child's bedroom in
house at 770 Fenwick Road, Bentley, Pennsylvania 00000

|  |  |
|---|---|
|  | $2,730.00 |
| Down payment received 5/21/2001 | −1,000.00 |
| Balance due | $1,730.00 |

■ **TERMS:**

In accordance with Letter Agreement of May 21, 2001,
and down payment of $1,000 credited.
Payment of this invoice is due within 30 days.
Thereafter, interest will accrue at the rate of 1½%
per month.

---

■ **TIP**

Always make it clear if the bill is a final bill and be certain that any
bill marked "Final" includes everything for which you intend to bill.
  Also, as noted on this sample, mention the letter agreement or
contract whenever possible in bills. This gives the bill a more official
look and increases the chances of prompt payment.

---

3. Bill monthly:   If a job lasts for more than one month, send
the owner a bill for work and materials to date (with credit
for any advance payment) every month without fail. If you
have a number of open jobs, pick a single day each month to
be the billing day. Contractors who don't bill for their work
for months at a time suffer nonpayments far in excess of
those who bill every month. The number of things that can
happen to an owner, to the job, or even to the contractor during a long period of time without billing is considerable.

4. Keep copies of your bills:   Chapter 4 goes into detail about
keeping your business records. Depending upon how big
your business is, you'll want to keep at least one copy of
your bill with your customer's file.

**What to include on the bill**   Every bill should explain the work that has been done and the materials supplied up to the date of that bill. If it takes a phone call or two to get the prices of materials, the time making those phone calls is well spent. A bill that accurately reflects the work that was done and the materials that were provided is believable to owners. These bills get paid before those that appear to be last-minute efforts to get money to keep cash flow moving. There are seven key items to include in your bill:

- Name of your company
- Name of your customer
- What you did/when/where (be as detailed as you need to be to avoid questions)
- List of materials and receipts
- Acknowledgment of credit for advance payment
- Balance due
- Date the balance is due

See the sample bills on pp. 20–21 for suggested wording.

## ■ Recording payments

Record all payments from customers as soon as you receive them. This is important so that you:

- Know how much you have been paid.
- Know how much more they owe.
- Have records of all bank deposits for your checkbook.
- Can follow up if a customer does not pay you when he should.

Chapter 4 covers the best way to keep track of that information.

## ■ What if a bill is not paid?

Just as timing is important when sending the bill to your customer, timing is essential if your customer doesn't pay when he should. There are four steps to take when this happens:

1. If the customer doesn't pay within the agreed-upon amount of time, send him a "friendly reminder" letter immediately—

■ **Calvin B. Olmstead**
**LICENSED PLUMBER**
88-A Watermain Avenue
Aquataine, Pennsylvania 00000
August 5, 2001

Mr. Stan N. Deepwater
7102 Marzipan Lane
Floodplain, Pennsylvania 00000

Dear Mr. Deepwater:

My invoice of June 30, 2001, remains unpaid. As indicated on the invoice, payment was required within 30 days.

I would appreciate your prompt remittance of the amount owed [so that work may continue on this job uninterrupted].

Sincerely,
Calvin B. Olmstead

■ **TIP**

If this invoice is for a final bill, do not include the words in brackets.

even if you're seeing the owner on a regular basis. As with your bills, this letter needs to be typed and neat. It should not be harsh or inappropriate, but it needs to be clear and firm. See the sample "friendly reminder" letter above. Don't worry about this type of letter chasing away good clients. Good clients expect contractors to do good work at reasonable prices and get paid for it.

2. Use this step only if you are still working for this customer. If you are still on the job and the customer has not responded to your reminder letter within one week, pack up your tools, remove the supplies from the job site, and stop work. Thirty days is long enough for anyone to pay his bills. If this was an honest oversight on the owner's part, your reminder letter should be enough to prompt the payment or at least an offer to pay. Do not continue working without payment. If you are finished with the job, go right to step 3.

3. If your customer has not paid at this point, write a final letter to the owner, advising him that the bill will be turned over for collection within one week. See the sample "final notice" letter below. Don't delay on this step. Bills that don't get paid after 30 days are very difficult to collect. If the customer doesn't pay, you have the choice of turning the matter over to a collections agency (lawyers are too expensive for most such bills) or writing off the bill.

---

■ **Calvin B. Olmstead**
**LICENSED PLUMBER**
88-A Watermain Avenue
Aquataine, Pennsylvania 00000
August 12, 2001

---

Ms. H. Tuo
6753 Drainy Cove Way
Sealevel, Pennsylvania 00000

Dear Ms. Tuo:

On August 5, 2001, I wrote to you noting that my invoice of June 30, 2001, was unpaid and the 30 days provided for payment had expired. I have had no response to my letter and the invoice remains unpaid.

Accordingly, I must regrettably advise you that I shall be forced to turn this matter over to collections authorities immediately. [In addition, I will not be able to continue work on this job.] [In addition, I intend to review with my advisor the appropriateness of filing a mechanic's lien to remedy the nonpayment.]

I very much regret the necessity for taking these actions and request, once again, that you pay this bill immediately.

Sincerely,
Calvin B. Olmstead

**■ TIP**

The threat to discontinue work is not appropriate if the unpaid bill is a final bill. The threat to file a mechanic's lien is subject to the matters discussed.

Always bear in mind that it is not lawful to threaten criminal action, reporting to public agencies, or other actions in any manner involving governments.

4. Consider a mechanic's lien. You may be able to do this in situations such as a substantial home or office renovation. If it is legally established, a mechanic's lien causes difficulties to owners with financing, possible sales, and similar matters. The laws of each state are different about mechanic's liens, and it will probably take you some effort to see whether your work falls within the scope of the law in your particular state. The reality is that mechanic's lien procedures are extremely difficult, even for attorneys. Unless a fairly substantial amount of money is involved or an attorney is willing to accept the matter on a completely contingent fee basis, a mechanic's lien is probably not a good option. However, your final letter should mention your possible intention to file a mechanic's lien within the time allotted by law. Just the mere mention of this possibility may shake a payment loose. Remember that it is not lawful to threaten criminal action, reporting to public agencies, or other actions involving governments. Private creditors are entitled to threaten to use lawful civil remedies only.

The sample final notice letter on the facing page contains in brackets an optional provision regarding a possible mechanic's lien.

You know which tools you need to do a professional job in your trade. Whether they are hammers, levels, meters, or any other tool, they are comfortable and familiar to you and you know that they help to make your work easier and look better. This book is about giving you tools—some large and some small—to help make it easier for your business to be financially successful. Tools such as pricing your work, accounting for all expenses, and billing and collecting are as essential to the business life of any contractor as a hammer is to a carpenter.

You will also find that once these new tools become familiar and comfortable to you, they won't be a drain on your time. In fact, they will give you more time and more money. These three tools—establishing hourly rate prices for your work, accounting for all expenses, and properly billing for your work—establish the framework for making your work as profitable as possible. Each chapter of this book fills your toolbox with another valuable tool that will form the basis of a fully professional small business that will give you the rewards that you deserve for long, hard hours of work.

# CHAPTER 2

# Putting It in Writing:
## Contracts and Beyond

**T**here's an old saying that goes, "Say what you mean and mean what you say." Adding a little spin to that, this chapter is about saying what you do and doing what you say: putting your agreement into writing, following through and following up, and dealing with problems quickly and (hopefully) with minimal pain.

*Confirm agreements to do work in writing even when the amount of work is very small.*

Before you begin work, you need to put your agreement in writing. Yes, it's so easy to say, "I don't have time for that paperwork. It's just legal mumbo jumbo. I want to get started on the real work." The fact is you don't have the time *not* to put your agreement in writing. Why risk losing a job, not getting paid, or waging an expensive and time-consuming legal battle simply because of a misunderstanding? This chapter will teach you how to use a few more tools for your "business toolbox." These new tools will help you make sure that there is a clear and legal understanding between you and the owner about what you're doing, when you are doing it, and how much and when he is paying you.

## Estimates and Contracts

You've carefully priced a job and spoken with the owner explaining exactly what you plan to do and the cost involved. He has given you the green light, and you're eager to get started. But before you do, you need to get the agreement in writing. You may first want to give the customer a written estimate and then a written contract to be signed, or you may feel you can bypass the estimate and simply prepare the contract. Either way is okay; the important thing is to confirm agreements to do work in writing even when the amount of work is very small.

## ■ Why a written contract?

There are three major reasons for written contracts:

- **AVOID MISUNDERSTANDING:**   People tend to hear what they want to hear and leave conversations with different views of what was agreed. You may think that you explained the job perfectly, but the owner can walk away with a very different view. A written agreement puts all the cards face up on the table and eliminates confusion about the scope of the work, the materials, and the price. If there is a misunderstanding, it's better to know about it now, before you have invested time in the project.

- **ADD LEGAL CLOUT:**   For every job, there is always the possibility that the owner will not pay for the work as agreed. This is one of a contractor's most common problems. With a written and signed agreement, you are stopping problems before they start. Most owners know that written agreements have greater legal force than verbal ones, and therefore they are more likely to pay you on time.

- **LOOK PROFESSIONAL AND BE TREATED THAT WAY:**   Your customers will take written agreements more seriously than simple verbal statements. A written agreement has an appearance that commands greater attention than the spoken word. Contractors who use written agreements are viewed as professionals (because they are) and treated accordingly (as they should be).

Written agreements may seem to be mere formalities but they are not. They are simple business tools that significantly increase your ability to work profitably.

### ■ Estimates vs. agreements/contracts

Depending upon the size of your business and the customer you are working with, you may first want to give your customer a written estimate or proposal. It's not much additional work to do an estimate first. All the information you'll put into the final contract first goes into the estimate. Once the customer has agreed to the estimate, it's a simple task to transfer the details from the estimate onto the contract. If you need to make some adjustments to the estimate, you'll include those in the contract.

---

**■ Malcolm O. Williams**
**STATE LINE CONSTRUCTION COMPANY, INC.**
5003 Forest Hill Drive
Woodchuck, Pennsylvania 00000
Phone: (333) 123-1234  Fax: (333) 123-1235
October 15, 2000

---

Ms. Frances P. Decker
4 Green Way
Patioville, Pennsylvania 00000

**■ ESTIMATE**

I estimate [This company estimates] that construction of a porch addition to your house at 4 Green Way, Patioville, Pennsylvania, in accordance with plans and specifications prepared by Franklin D. Smyth, Architect, which you have reviewed with me, will be $12,486. This estimate does not include obtaining building and electrical permits for this work.

This is not a contract or an offer to enter into a contract. It is for our mutual convenience in considering a possible contract.

This estimate is based on current market prices of necessary materials and present rates for the labor that will be required. Accordingly, this estimate will need to be revised if you decide not to enter a contract with me [this company] within the next 30 days.

I [This company] would be pleased to discuss this estimate with you at your convenience.

Sincerely,
Malcolm O. Williams

The major difference between the estimate and the contract is that estimates provide information to the customer, while the contract is a legal agreement that binds you and the owner to the terms. Throughout this chapter, I'll use the terms "agreement" and "contract" interchangeably. For what I'm covering here, they mean the same thing. Comments about contracts/agreements generally apply also to estimates.

There are two basic types of contracts that you'll be working with:

- **CONTRACTS YOU CREATE:** You'll use these most of the time. Unless the job is very complex, you can easily and economically prepare contracts that are effective.

- **PREPARED CONTRACTS:** These are used for major projects and are normally supplied by owners or general contractors.

## ■ Writing your contract

In most cases, your contract can simply be a confirming letter carefully typed on your letterhead. (You can also use standard forms that you'll find in most office-supply stores.) It may be just a few sentences, but there are two main points that you must cover:

- Scope of the work

- Payment arrangement

The sample letter shown on p. 30 works fine for the majority of contracts. When you describe the work, be very clear and precise because the clearer you are now, the better. The same is true for the payment terms. Tell your customer exactly how much the job will cost, the amount of the down payment and when it's due, as well as the balance. See the checklist above for details on preparing the contract.

---

**What to List in Your Contract**

❏ Work to be done
❏ Plans, specifications, and other documents involved in the work
❏ Allowances
❏ Cost of job
❏ Advance payment
❏ Payment schedule for the balance of the work
❏ Work that is not included in the agreement
❏ Materials you will get
❏ Materials you will not get
❏ Who will be responsible for obtaining permits
❏ When the work will begin
❏ When the work will be finished

---

**What to Do with the Contract**

❏ Make two copies.
❏ Ask the owner to sign a copy and return it to you.
❏ Collect advance payment when the owner signs.

■ **Frank G. Powermain**
**LICENSED ELECTRICIAN**
1985 Seersucker Lane
Bolton, Pennsylvania 00000
Phone: (777) 123-1234  Fax: (777) 123-1235
July 15, 2000

■ **LETTER OF AGREEMENT**

Mr. Marvin Airflower
4433 Windy Gap Lane
Cloudsville, Pennsylvania 00000

Dear Mr. Airflower:

I am pleased to confirm that I [company] have [has] agreed to install three through-the-wall Friedrich air-conditioner units (to be supplied by owner) in the three bedrooms of your house at 4433 Windy Gap Lane, Cloudsville, Pennsylvania. The work will include installation of necessary receptacles for all three air conditioners, including a 220-volt receptacle for the unit in the large bedroom. The work will also include painting, both inside and outside.

The total price for the work will be $1,628. Upon signing of this agreement, $750 is due and must be paid in advance of work beginning. The balance ($878) will be paid upon completion and presentation of my [our] bill. The balance will be billed upon completion of the work and is due within 30 days.

This work will be completed by August 20, 2000.*

I appreciate the opportunity to perform this work. Please sign the enclosed copy of this letter and return it to me along with your advance payment. This will confirm our agreement regarding the work.

Sincerely,

_____
Date                          Frank G. Powermain

_____
Date                          Marvin Airflower

*The $750 deposit must be received before work will begin. If start of work is delayed, finish date will necessarily change.

### ▇ TIP

- The letter of agreement on the facing page specifically states that the air-conditioning units are not to be supplied by the contractor. The remaining items, including outlets, wiring, trim wood, paint, and so forth, would be supplied by the contractor.
- You don't need to write these letters of agreement in any sort of formal language. In fact, don't try to copy legal language that you may have heard or read. Simply write what has been agreed to in plain, understandable English.
- Since this letter of agreement does not state otherwise, it is assumed that the cost of materials will not be advanced, except what may be included in the agreed advance payment. Be sure that the initial payment is sufficient to cover the cost of materials or you will be forced to pay for those out-of-pocket.
- Be sure that your subcontractors understand the payment schedule and agree to await their payments until you are paid.

These two items, scope of work and payment terms, are all that you need to include most of the time. There are, however, other points that may come up from time to time. You may need to include one or more of the following additional items:

- **EXCLUSIONS:**  Are there any features or tasks that are not included in your job? If so, be sure to list these carefully. These might include leaving drywall or woodwork unpainted, or there may be materials that the owner is responsible for obtaining at his own expense.  There are contracts that don't include plumbing and electrical fixtures and other such items. These items may need to be paid for by the owner even though the contractor picks them up with the other supplies.

- **PERMITS:**  If permits (such as building and electrical) are involved in the job, include a line that tells who is responsible for getting them. Without a definite statement one way or the other, it's unclear who is responsible. You don't want to be in a position where the owner will argue that you are responsible when you aren't. Look at the agreement between Malcolm Williams and Frances Decker on p. 32. Malcolm was very clear about who was responsible for getting the building and electrical permits.

### Including the Exclusions

Jim, a carpenter, is building a one-room addition to Pete's home. Pete is pretty handy and wants to save some money, so he told Jim that he wants to do all of the painting and staining. Jim makes an adjustment in his price and when he describes the work in his contract, he adds a separate line stating that all the walls and woodwork will be left unfinished. If Pete should forget what they had agreed to, he can't go back to Jim and demand that Jim do the painting and staining.

■ **Malcolm O. Williams**
**STATE LINE CONSTRUCTION COMPANY, INC.**
5003 Forest Hill Drive
Woodchuck, Pennsylvania 00000
Phone: (333) 123-1234  Fax: (333) 123-1235
August 1, 2000

■ **LETTER OF AGREEMENT**

Ms. Frances P. Decker
4 Green Way
Patioville, Pennsylvania 00000

Dear Ms. Decker:

This letter will confirm my [company's] agreement to construct a porch addition to your residence at 4 Green Way, Patioville, Pennsylvania, in accordance with plans and specifications prepared by Franklin D. Smythe, Architect. You will be responsible for obtaining the building and electrical permits for this work. Work will be completed no later than November 15, 2000.*

This work will be performed and materials furnished for the price of $12,486. Upon signing of contract, $4,000 is due and must be paid prior to beginning work; $4,000 is due at the time of completion of the foundation and floor; and $2,000 is due at the time rough-in is completed and the porch is under roof. The balance ($2,486) is due at the time all work is completed. I will bill you in accordance with this payment schedule, and payment is required within 30 days.

I appreciate the opportunity to perform this work. Please sign the enclosed copy of this letter and return it to me. This will confirm our agreement regarding the work.

Sincerely,

Malcolm O. Williams [for State Line Construction Company, Inc.]

_____
Date                                    Frances P. Decker

*The $4,000 deposit must be received before work will begin. If start of work is delayed, finish date will necessarily change.

**TIP**

This letter of agreement removes from the contractor the responsibility for getting permits. Even when written this way, it may be in your interest to get the permit or assist the owner in doing so. You will probably get the permit more easily and more quickly than the owner and can get started with your work. Nevertheless, the responsibility is removed from your shoulders by a letter such as this.

- **LENGTH OF TIME FOR JOB:** If you expect that the job will take longer than it might normally take, be sure to mention that clearly in the agreement. It is assumed when a written agreement does not specifically state a time of completion that the work will be completed in a "reasonable" time. Obviously, "reasonable" can mean many things, and consequently there are often disputes about this. Be on the safe side. Put in the letter the length of time you will need to complete the job, remembering that things typically take longer than you expect.

- **PLANS TO BE USED:** If the work you are hired to do is described in plans or any other documents, refer to them in your letter of agreement. Include the names and numbers of the plans or some form of identification so that it's clear which plans you mean. If there is anything in the plans or documents that differs from the work you agreed to do, be sure to mention that, too. While plans and documents are extremely useful in confirming agreements to do work, they must accurately reflect what you have agreed to do.

- **ALLOWANCES:** If there are any allowances in your agreement, describe them clearly and give the exact dollar amount of the allowance. Allowances are used when you don't know the exact cost of an item or when the customer has the option of selecting a higher-quality, more expensive type of an item. Tell the customer what you expect the cost to be and include a statement that if the cost goes up, so will the price.

- **TAKEOFFS:** If you're a subcontractor and are entering a contract with a general contractor, you will be responsible for only some of the work shown on the general plans. For example, an owner may have a contract with a general contractor to build his house. As a plumbing subcontractor, you must

### Don't Guess at Takeoffs

Stu is a plumbing subcontractor. He had an opportunity to bid for the plumbing portion of a general contractor's extensive renovation job at the Henderson house. Stu didn't do his takeoff carefully, but unfortunately he got the job. The contract required him to do "all plumbing work as reflected in the plans and specifications of June 23, 2001, of Chester P. Adams, Architect." In his careless takeoff, Stu picked up all of the bathroom work on the plans and specifications but failed to notice the kitchen and utility room work. Stu ended up working six days for free! He was lucky that his contract did not require him to furnish the fixtures as well.

determine your work from the general plans by doing a take-off. A takeoff is your determination of exactly what part of the work indicated on the general plans is your responsibility. Since you are a plumber, your work would include all pipes, drains, bathroom and kitchen fixtures, and so on.

Since each contract you enter must describe exactly what you have agreed to do, you shouldn't enter a contract with a general contractor or with an owner based upon general plans until you're certain that your takeoff is correct. The description of work in your contract will be something like "the provision of all plumbing work shown on plans and specifications of July 19, 2001, of John Smith, Architect, in a workmanlike fashion including all necessary supplies and fixtures and cleanup." A subcontractor who enters such a contract and prices the job based upon an erroneous takeoff will bear the loss. Don't guess about takeoffs: It will ultimately cost you money if you do.

*The fine print matters. If you don't understand something in a contract, you need to talk with someone who does.*

## ■ Working with complex contracts

There are times when a job is too complex for the contract to be confirmed in the simple letter of agreement described above. In most of these situations, the general contractor or owner hiring you will provide a form contract for you. Often this is a standard contract, such as an American Institute of Architects (AIA) contract. These contracts can be long, complex, and frankly, pretty frightening. You may need to have a lawyer help you with them. Here are a few rules to follow when working with complex contracts and lawyers:

1. **DON'T SIGN IT IF YOU DON'T UNDERSTAND IT:** Never sign a contract if there is any substantial matter that you don't understand. Don't fall into the trap of saying, "This is just legalese and the fine print doesn't matter." Yes, it's a fair assumption that long, lawyerly agreements that are prepared by the other party are not written to benefit you. But that doesn't excuse you from reading and understanding what you're agreeing to. The fine print matters. If you don't understand something in a contract, you need to talk with someone who does.

2. **SEE A LAWYER IF YOU NEED TO:**  Although lawyers can be expensive and you'll find only a few instances in this book where I'll recommend one, this is one of those times. Chapter 6 describes the best way to find a good lawyer. You need one who is willing to work with you on a limited basis. A complex contract justifies an hour or two of legal advice, but this will only be worth your money if you prepare for it properly.

3. **DO YOUR HOMEWORK BEFORE YOU SEE A LAWYER:**  Spell out very carefully what it is you want your lawyer to do. You should make it clear to the lawyer that you wish to engage him for the limited purpose of explaining just certain items to you—not to review the entire contract. If you give the lawyer a complicated construction contract and no directions that tell him what you want him to do, the lawyer will probably review the entire contract, all the documents that are referred to in the contract, the plans, as well as other materials. This will take a lot of time and money and isn't what you need. To avoid this, review the contract yourself and highlight those areas that you don't understand or where you need help. For example, if the description of the work is acceptable and you have no doubt about your understanding of it, the lawyer need not spend time (and your money) reviewing it.

4. **FIND OUT WHAT YOU ARE MISSING:**  Ask your lawyer to look for issues in the contract that might be legal pitfalls that a layperson wouldn't recognize. These are potential problems that should leap off the page for most lawyers who are familiar with construction contracts, which is the type of lawyer you should use. This should not involve much additional time and cost to you—especially if the contract is a form agreement such as an AIA contract. A lawyer who works in the construction area has probably seen most forms many times.

## Following through after the Contract

You surely know by now that this book isn't about how to do your job. It's about what you can and should do behind the scenes so that the time and effort that you spend in your job is as good and effective as it can be. Falling into that category are actions you need to do as follow-through once the contract is signed. These include:

- Scheduling
- Collecting the advance payment
- Ordering the supplies
- Billing during the job (if it's a long job)
- Communicating with the owner

## Scheduling

This may seem too simple to say, but it's essential. Unless you have a very simple work life or an unusual memory, you need to plan the timing of your jobs to allow enough days for each one so that they don't overlap unexpectedly (see pp. 49–54).

## Collecting the advance payment

Unless the owner hands you a check immediately, send a bill for any advance payment immediately after an agreement is signed (see pp. 19–22 on preparing the bill). The bill for advance payments should be due upon receipt.

## Ordering the supplies

Order the necessary supplies as soon as you can after the contract is signed to be certain that the prices are locked in at the price you quoted the owner. Timing can be touchy here. If the owner has agreed to an advance payment—particularly if the advance covers all or part of the materials—you should have that cash in hand before ordering the supplies.

If you need to store materials at the owner's site, discuss this with the owner immediately and work out an acceptable delivery schedule. This shouldn't be a problem since most owners understand that contractors need sufficient use of the site to do the work and to store a reasonable amount of the necessary materials and tools. Nevertheless, as I'll mention in the next section, it's always best to keep clear communication with the owners to maintain the best possible relationship.

## ■ Billing during the job

The terms of your contract require you to do the work properly and on time. The contract also requires the owner to pay you fully and on time. Payment is not optional, nor is billing. If you are working on a long job, you need to take the time to send bills monthly for work and materials. It's not easy to take a tough stand on payment, but it's surely easier than working without getting paid. You don't have the luxury of working in good faith on an owner's promise to pay. You need to pay your bills on time, and so do your customers. If they don't, stop work and follow the suggestions in chapter 1 about reminder letters, final demand letters, and collection companies.

## ■ Communicating with the owner

Just as clear communication with the owner is vital when you're estimating the job, it's equally important to keep in contact with the owner once the work is under way. During the course of the job, give the owner progress reports. It's a good way to keep communication open, keep owners up to date on how things are going, and let them be involved. This is more than just a mere courtesy; it's good business practice. If the owners are a part of their projects and they have

---

### Nonpayment Is Nonpayment, Plain and Simple

Henry, a painter, has taken a job to paint the interior of a six-room house for $2,775, paint included. His contract with the owner calls for a $1,000 deposit, which the owner paid, $1,000 when four of the six rooms are painted, and $775 when done. Henry finished the first four rooms in a week and sent the owner a bill for the second $1,000 payment. The owner asked him to take a break from the painting to work on another job.

By the time he finished the other job and was able to return to the painting, 30 days had passed and he had not yet been paid the $1,000 that should have been paid. Instead of painting the rest of the rooms, Henry sent a reminder letter to the owner and stopped painting. Henry knew that once he finished the living and dining rooms, he would have no leverage to force the owner to pay. In addition, since the owner was delaying making a $1,000 payment in the middle of the job, he would almost certainly delay in making the final payment of $775.

*The contractor who completes the work almost invisibly often finds himself "out of sight, out of mind" when he sends his bill.*

an opportunity to get to know you a bit, they are more likely to be satisfied with the work and pay your bills right away. The contractor who completes the work almost invisibly often finds himself "out of sight, out of mind" when he sends his bill.

Check in with the owner at least once during the job—even on the smallest job. For example, in the through-the-wall air-conditioning contract between Marvin Airflower and Frank G. Powermain on p. 30, there is almost nothing to check. The air conditioners have been picked out and their proposed locations are marked. Frank could, however, show Mr. Airflower the trim he proposes to use around the air conditioners once they are installed in the wall. While this is not a very big point to discuss, Mr. Airflower will appreciate Frank's raising it and tend not to make a fuss about other items if he is not entirely happy.

## ▄Contract Disputes

Having a written and signed contract will prevent most common problems, but, unfortunately, contracts are not bulletproof. Problems can and do come up and fall into three general categories:

- Simple changes or adjustments to the plan
- Moderate disputes
- Major disputes

### ■ When a job calls for changes

Once you get into a job, you sometimes see new situations that you couldn't have seen before starting it. Sometimes you see a better way to do what the owner wants and can suggest changes that will make the job easier and maybe save the owner money—that's the good news. But there are also times when you find you can't do the job exactly as you had agreed in the contract—that's the bad news. Either way, good or bad, talk to the owner about it immediately. As you would expect, owners are always grateful for advice about a better or less expensive way to accomplish something. But on the other side of the coin, most owners are reasonable and understand that un-foreseen situations can develop that prevent you from doing the work exactly as you had both expected.

The key here is to talk with the owner. Give him a full and accu-rate description of the situation, offer reasonable alternatives to what is in the contract, and show him the benefits and drawbacks of the alternatives. Don't tell him about the problem without offering a good and reasonable solution. By offering a solution, you can most likely handle the change in plans and keep your customer happy.

If the change involves the appearance of a job, it is particularly important to discuss this change with the owner. People fix mental images of things in their minds and stick with them even when some-thing else is equally attractive and appropriate. This isn't the sort of thing an owner will change easily.

### Good News, Bad News

Pete, an electrician, delivered the good news. He was working on the Johnson house, circa 1920, with solid plaster walls. Even though the plans in the contract called for hardwired wall switches, he suggested changing to wireless switches. Pete knew that the hardwired switches would be a major (and costly) undertaking. The wireless switches, on the other hand, required a very small investment, could be mounted on a control about the size of a television remote, and could be placed anywhere and moved at any time. Mr. Johnson was delighted to save some money.

Dan, a plumber, was stuck telling the bad news. He, too, was working on the Johnson house and was supposed to install an expensive and uniquely styled toilet. Although the distributor claimed it was available when Dan prepared the contract, he found that it was now out of production and impossible to get. Fortunately, Dan did his homework before talking about this problem with Mr. Johnson. He was able to locate a similar model from a different manufacturer at a slightly higher price. As you can imagine, Mr. Johnson didn't want to hear that his precious $1,500 low-slung, one-piece toilet was no longer available and that Dan would substitute a standard-height, two-piece model that sells for $139.95.

## ▪ Resolving moderate disputes

Having a written agreement eliminates most misunderstandings, but unfortunately, even the best, well-thought-out, thoroughly discussed contracts sometimes do not prevent disputes between the owner and contractor. This often occurs when something outside of your control interrupts the work plans, such as when:

- You can't complete your work within the time agreed because the work of another party or even the owner's own actions make this impossible.

- You can't use the materials that you included in your agreement because they are no longer available.

- You need to make a change that will look different from what was called for in the agreement.

- A contract requires something that turns out to be impossible in light of factors that emerge as the work proceeds. Excavation contractors deal with this regularly when large amounts of sub-surface rock keep them from digging a foundation.

If possible, use the contract to resolve the dispute. Looking more carefully at the contract is the quickest and least expensive way to resolve disputes if owner and contractor can agree to it. Very often, a fresh look at the precise language of a contract and the plans and specifications for the work will shed new light on the disputed matter. If you can discuss a matter with an owner and agree that you will look together at the contract to see if it resolves the dispute, you're well on your way to a solution. If the owner has already involved his attorney, this approach probably won't work.

**What are your legal rights?** In most situations, an open and honest conversation with the owner will resolve the problem. However, if the owner is difficult when you are discussing this, it may be helpful to know what your legal rights are. Although the laws of each state differ to some extent, there are general principles of law that are used in every state in some fashion:

- **IMPOSSIBILITY:** In general, the law is reasonable regarding most issues that arise in contracts for work that are not specifically addressed in the contract. For example, when it

*Looking more carefully at the contract is the quickest and least expensive way to resolve disputes if owner and contractor can agree to it.*

becomes impossible to provide the precise materials called for in plans and specifications because those materials are simply unavailable, the law excuses the contractor as long as he makes every attempt to provide the best possible substitute. According to the law in most states, "impossibility" is generally recognized as an excuse for precise performance even when it is not mentioned specifically in the contract.

- **SUBSTANTIAL PERFORMANCE:** Another example of the law's reasonableness is the concept of "substantial performance." In general, the law does not require pointlessly technical following of plans and specifications if the work has taken place in good faith and it is nearly but not absolutely as indicated. But substantial performance doesn't give you permission to deviate from plans without a good reason. If an owner's plans call for a particular item that is available and can do what the plans intend it to do, the contractor must use that item even if he feels that a substitute is just as good in every respect.

## ■ Handling major disputes

Sometimes the contract and discussions with the owner just aren't enough. The owner is still unhappy and there is no resolution in sight. What's next?

**Stop work and confirm the dispute in writing** If your discussions are getting nowhere and it's now likely that the owner won't pay you for your work, stop working on the job and write a letter confirming what you are doing and why. Send this letter certified mail with a return receipt requested (your post office will show you how to do this). See the letter on p. 42 that Terry Kotta wrote to Ms. Bloch about the dispute over brickwork. As you can see, Mr. Kotta has carefully described the dispute he's having with Ms. Bloch and suggested ways to resolve it. He has also carefully explained why he's taking the action he has chosen.

Sending a letter has two purposes:

- It states exactly what your position is and may be important later if this matter ends up in court. In Terry's situation, Ms. Bloch won't be able to claim that Terry stopped working for any other reason than the unresolved dispute.

■ **Terry Kotta**
**BRICKMAN & ASSOCIATES**
P.O. Box 62
Feldspar, Virginia 00000
Phone: (555) 123-1234  Fax: (555) 123-1235
July 27, 2000

CERTIFIED MAIL
RETURN RECEIPT REQUESTED

Ms. Cindy R. Bloch
734 Winding Walk Way
Wallflower, Virginia 00000

Dear Ms. Bloch:

I regret having to write this letter, but it appears as though an important difference of opinion has arisen.

In my view, the brickwork that has been completed on the south wall of the building is precisely what is called for in the contract. In addition, you expressly approved the layup the mason prepared prior to making the wall. The bricks and grout are precisely the same as were used in the layup. I also feel that the pointing is workmanlike in every respect.

You are apparently of the view that the grout does not match the grout called for in the contract and approved by you and that the pointing is not satisfactory. I am prepared to prove to you that the grout is precisely the same as approved in the layup. As to the pointing, I am prepared to submit the matter to a professional mason of our mutual choosing and permit him to make a judgment as to whether the work is satisfactory. I suggest that we do these things promptly.

In light of this significant difference of opinion, I am not going to continue work until the matter is resolved. I hope that you can understand my reason for this.

Please let me hear from you with regard to this matter at your earliest convenience.

Sincerely,

Terry Kotta

- When owners see that you are handling a dispute in a professional manner and they realize that you will not finish the job without resolving the matter, they may reconsider their position and become more reasonable. If Ms. Bloch's

**TIP**

- The type of letter on the facing page should describe the controversy and make clear your position.
- If you are stopping work on the project, say that very clearly.
- When you are able to suggest a solution, such as the use of an outside mason to examine the pointing, mention that in this letter. This not only gives a possibility for resolution but also shows that you are actively working for a resolution.

lawyer sees a letter confirming that you have stopped work for a good-faith reason and that you have suggested a reasonable solution, it's possible that he would encourage her to resolve the matter with you. He might suggest that she hire another contractor to finish the job and release you from further responsibility.

**Legal action or no action**    If a letter doesn't resolve the situation, the next step, unfortunately, would be to hire a lawyer to assist you (see the guidelines on pp. 109–112 for hiring a lawyer). However, before you take that step, carefully consider whether you have enough to gain by it. At a minimum, hiring a lawyer means paying that lawyer's fee and losing many hours of billable time that you'll spend working with the lawyer. It's also fair to say that legal battles are not pleasant experiences. Never take a legal action because you feel that it's "a matter of principle." You're a businessperson. It's a matter of money and nothing else.

*Never take a legal action because you feel that it's "a matter of principle." You're a businessperson. It's a matter of money and nothing else.*

One realistic possibility, depending upon how much the owner still owes you, is to leave the work unfinished and let your letter stand as your final position in the matter. As long as you have made it understood that you will not resume work until the dispute is resolved, your position would be clear in any legal proceeding the owner might bring. Lawsuits to force contractors to do work are usually not a good choice for the owner. Courts will generally not require a contractor to finish the job. An owner who simply wants to get the job completed at the price he agreed to will often conclude that it's best to settle with the contractor who has stopped work and hire someone else to finish the job.

▓▓ **TIP**

**A BUSY CONTRACTOR FRIEND TOLD ME**

"I find that my customers take me more seriously and pay me quicker with less discussion when I give them a professional-looking, written contract to sign before I begin work."

Written contracts are good housekeeping for contractors. They are like safety measures for your business. Contracts take a little more time, but the financial protection that you gain is more than worth the effort. Just as goggles protect a carpenter's eyes when sawing, your written contract protects your financial situation.

In addition to the contract, scheduling, billing, and communication with the owner are key tools that help the job move smoothly and result in greater customer satisfaction. If you do these things on every job, you will find that the process becomes easier and easier and, sooner or later, almost automatic. Contractors who have done these things will tell you that they receive better compensation for their work and easier payment of their bills than they could ever expect without doing them.

If a job doesn't go smoothly, you are not powerless. You have tools that will help you to resolve the dispute with the least amount of difficulty and expense. You might choose to work with a lawyer, but you may also find that because you have a solid contract on your side—and the owner knows that—you can avoid that expense.

# CHAPTER 3

# Running and Growing Your Business

**C**hapters 1 and 2 covered pricing your work and creating contracts. But once a contract is signed, your work has really just begun, both in terms of the work at the job sites and in terms of running your business. You want each job to go as smoothly as possible, and you want more work after each job is done. There are three primary steps to running and growing your business:

1. Do quality work.

2. Keep jobs on schedule.

3. Keep in touch with your customers—current, past, and future.

You are in charge of the quality-work part—this book won't try to tell you how to do that. You already know that a job well done is your best advertisement to keep your customers coming back and to bring in new customers. But doing quality work isn't enough. What makes the difference between success and failure may have nothing to do with the quality of the work you do. Look at any two contractors. Even though they both do wonderful work, one is succeeding in his business and making a decent living, while the other is continually struggling with a late job, later payments from customers, and stacks of overdue bills. What makes the difference between these two workers? One big difference is how well organized their businesses are. You want to make sure that you're in the first group.

This chapter covers those tools that you need to keep your jobs on schedule and to keep communication clear between you, your customers, your fellow workers, and your suppliers. At the risk of sounding corny, you already know how to work hard. I'll show you how to work smart so that you can spend more time working on jobs and making money and less time with paperwork. I'll also cover ways to use your good work and your current customers to expand your business.

## Setting Up Your Office

The term "office" may seem strange to you—particularly if you are a small contractor. You probably think of your truck as your office. Try to think about "office" not so much as a space or location but as a state of mind. Your office is where you do most of the things that you need to do to run your business, other than working at the job site. Throughout this book, I talk about tasks that you do in running your business to make it more profitable. I've already talked about estimates and contracts and sending bills and follow-up bills to your customers, and I'll be discussing more. Whether your office is a spare bedroom, a rented office, or just the kitchen table after dinner, there are a few essentials you will need.

### ■ Essential equipment

When buying office equipment, keep it simple. You can run a good business, look big and respectable to the outside world, and, most important, stay very profitable by investing in a few business essentials. These include a phone and a separate phone/fax line, cell phone, fax/copy machine, answering machine or voice mail, typewriter or computer, post-office box, stationery and business cards, and a calendar (see the "Office Survival Kit" at left for a more complete listing).

While prices vary across the country, most of the following

---

**Office Survival Kit: What Do You Really Need?**

- ❏ Phone
- ❏ Cell phone
- ❏ Separate phone/fax line
- ❏ Answering machine or voice mail
- ❏ File cabinet or storage boxes
- ❏ Manila folders
- ❏ Typewriter or computer
- ❏ Fax/copy machine, toner cartridges
- ❏ Calculator
- ❏ Paper, pencils, pens, clips, stapler, staples
- ❏ Month-at-a-glance-style calendar
- ❏ Small postal scale and stamps
- ❏ Stationery, bill heads, envelopes, business cards

items should not be very expensive. I've included typical costs for some of these essentials, just to give you a ballpark number. And these items should be fully deductible on your income tax return; check with your accountant.

- **PHONE/FAX LINE:** You may work out of your home and use your kitchen table for your office, but your customers don't need to know that you are still small. By using your own phone line for your business, you are telling your customers that you are a professional and this is your full-time occupation, not just something that you do in your spare time. Keep this line for business only. You appear less than professional if a new customer calls and a young child answers the phone or if the phone is always busy. A phone line doesn't need to be expensive. Don't worry about the frills like caller ID or call forwarding; just get basic service for now. Cost: less than $50 per month plus a one-time installation fee.

- **FAX MACHINE:** A fax machine not only lets you send and receive information very quickly but can also be like an alternative answering machine when you aren't there. On the outgoing message of your answering machine, simply tell callers that they can fax information to the same number if they wish. In many cases, this will eliminate the need for returning the phone call, since many callers are able to accomplish what they intend by means of a fax.

  You don't need another phone line for your fax machine. Your local electronics store has line splitters so that your phone and fax can easily share the same line. Of course, you'll be able to send and receive all sorts of information such as prices of subcontractors, material suppliers, schedules for work, supply orders, and even correspondence to owners and contractors. When choosing your fax, make sure that it doubles as a copier. You should be able to find either new or used fax machines for less than $200.

- **CELL PHONE:** A cell phone can be a lifesaver for picking up your messages when you are out of the office and for returning calls during the day. It's practically a necessity today. But

> **Phone Essentials**
> - Get your own phone/ fax line.
> - Don't share your phone with your family.
> - Use an answering machine or voice mail.
> - Make sure you can check your messages when you're away from the office.
> - Get a cell phone.

it can be a mixed blessing if you don't turn it off when you are on the job or in important meetings.

- **ANSWERING MACHINE:**  There are several options here: answering machine, answering service, or voice mail through your phone company. You can get answering machines for less than $30 or add voice mail to your telephone service for about $8 a month. Whichever you choose, make sure that you can check your messages when you are away from home or the office. Of course, when you do get your messages, write them down so that you don't forget to call back.

- **TYPEWRITER:**  You don't need anything slick or fancy, but you do need to type your bills, contracts, and letters. If you don't have a typewriter hidden in a closet somewhere in your house, you might consider a computer instead. More on that in the next section.

- **POST-OFFICE BOX:**  Rent a post-office box and use that address on all of your correspondence. Unless your post office is very far away and checking your mail is therefore very time-consuming, having a post-office box gives your company a more substantial look and it prevents your business mail from accidentally getting mixed up with the family mail. The cost is typically $5 to $10 per month.

- **STATIONERY AND BUSINESS CARDS:**  Your local quick-print company can print letterhead, bill head, envelopes, and business cards with your company name, address, phone, fax, and e-mail on them. If you invest in a computer, you might be able to do these yourself. Always keep a supply of business cards in your wallet. You never know when you might need one.

- **CALENDAR:**  Get a large, month-at-a-glance-style calendar that you'll keep in your office and use for scheduling and reminders. Cost: about $10.

## ■ Using a computer

You can get by quite nicely with the essentials above, but you'll find that having a computer will more than pay for itself with the time it will save you. A computer may seem like a big investment and surely a tool that's very different from the ones you may be used to, but if there's any machine that can make your office life easier, this is it. You don't need the top of the line. You can pick up an older, refurbished model, although the prices of new computers are getting so competitive, you should look at them, too. You should be able to pick up a brand new PC with everything that you need (including a printer) for less than $1,000. Look for sales at your local computer warehouse store. There are two major ways in which you'll use a computer:

- Using word-processing software to quickly prepare your bills, letters, and reminders

- Using accounting software to help you keep your records and prepare your bills

In addition to these basic uses, you might want to have an e-mail account so that people can reach you over the Internet. If you have never used a computer before, there are many good books at your local bookstore or library to help you get started.

## Working Smart

You have your office set up, whether it's a room in your home or just a briefcase and laptop computer that you carry around. Now it's time to use it for three important tasks in running a profitable contracting business:

- Planning

- Scheduling

- Staying in touch

### Planning

Planning is as important to a job as doing the job itself. And good planning is a key part of making as much money as possible. Contractors who plan the time they will use to do particular jobs and who stick to their plans make more money for several reasons:

- **LESS WASTED TIME:** The key to making money as a contractor is to spend as many of your waking hours as possible doing work for which you can charge.

- **FEWER DELAYS:** Good planning and scheduling can help prevent unnecessary and costly delays. Planning means that the materials and people involved in a job will be where they are supposed to be when they are supposed to be there. The contractor who spends a serious hour after dinner on Sunday planning for the next week's work may save an hour or more of down time each day.

- **CREDIBILITY AND CONFIDENCE:** When you plan your work and follow through as you promised, your customers believe in your abilities and have more confidence in you. This credi-

---

**Q: Does planning really make money?**

**A:** Do you doubt that good planning is really worth the effort? Jim, a local plumber doesn't. Jim was scheduled to start remodeling Mr. Downwind's bathroom on Wednesday. He ordered the new fixtures a few weeks ago, and the distributor guaranteed that they would be delivered no later than Monday. When Jim arrived at Mr. Downwind's house at 8:00 A.M. on Wednesday, only the barking dog in the yard greeted him. Mr. Downwind had written down the wrong day. Jim went to a pay phone, called him at the office, and had a cup of coffee and a doughnut while he waited.

At 10:00 A.M., Mr. Downwind pulled up to let him in. Two hours wasted from his day, but that's only part of the problem. Once he got in, he realized that the fixtures hadn't been delivered as promised. Fortunately, the distributor put them right on a truck and they arrived by noon. Jim got started around 12:30 P.M.

What if he had invested an hour Sunday night to plan the week? Looking at his calendar, Jim would have seen that he had the job on Wednesday, would have called Mr. Downwind then to confirm, and would have made a note on his calendar to call the plumbing distributor first thing Monday. These few minutes could have saved him four hours of work.

Here's the math: Jim charges $40 per hour. Wednesday morning cost him $160 (plus the coffee and doughnut). And that was just one day. Being conservative, good planning could save one hour each day. That's 260 hours a year, or $10,400. Can you really afford not to plan?

bility results in more work. Customers assume that contractors who plan when they will do things and do them when planned will also perform other aspects of their work correctly.

- **INCOME PROTECTION:** By planning and scheduling, you can see very clearly if you are working (billing) the number of hours each week that you need to earn the income you want.

If your job involves other contractors or suppliers, it's especially important to plan and follow up. Your customer has a contract with you, not with the lumberyard. If you say that floor planks will be delivered on Tuesday but they're not, it really doesn't matter to the customer whether it was the lumberyard's fault. If they heard it from you, it's your responsibility.

Set aside an hour each week to plan your work for the following week. Many contractors do this Sunday night or sometime over the weekend so that they have their week organized when Monday morning rolls around. It's not as important when you do it—what's important is that you do it on a regular basis and that it becomes a habit. You can't afford not to plan.

*Set aside an hour each week to plan your work for the following week.*

## ■ Scheduling: use your calendar

Accurate scheduling of work is one of the most important requirements for service providers. People who hire contractors have the same questions about scheduling as do people who hire lawyers and accountants: "When will you get to it? When will it be finished?" The answers often determine whether you get the job in the first place.

There is a temptation to tell your customers what you think they want to hear, whether or not it's really possible. Believe it or not, they want the truth—nothing more. An owner likes to feel that the contractor he is hiring is in control of scheduling and can be relied upon to start and finish the job when he says he will do so. While there are factors that you can't control, there is much that you can do to make and keep a schedule.

The first step is so simple, it sounds almost silly: Use a calendar. You'd be surprised how many people don't do it. The important word here is *use*. It's easy to buy a calendar but to force yourself to use it and rely upon it takes some practice. If you don't already have one,

## SEPTEMBER 2000

| SUNDAY | MONDAY | TUESDAY | WEDNESDAY | THURSDAY | FRIDAY | SATURDAY |
|---|---|---|---|---|---|---|
| | | | | | **1** Pick up supplies for Harrington job 2:00—Meet with Mr. Harrington to discuss site preparation and job in general | **2** Repair items for William and Brown jobs |
| **3** Call McGinnis re: 9/4 job | **4** 9:00-12:00— McGinnis—Install lolly columns in basement 5:00—Bob's cookout | **5** 8:00-11:00— First day of school! Harrington job all day McGinnis— send final bill | **6** Harrington job all day | **7** Harrington job all day Pick up cabinets for Beckwith job | **8** 9:00-11:00— Finish Harrington job | **9** Jones repair job |
| **10** Call Ms. Beckwith re: 9/11 start-up date Call Mr. Stern re: 9/14 job | **11** Beckwith kitchen job all day Send Jones and Harrington bills | **12** Beckwith kitchen job all day Pick up materials for Stern job | **13** 9:00-2:00— Beckwith kitchen job | **14** Stern floor job Call Dave Smith about possible shelving job discussed last week | **15** 9:00-3:00— Stern floor job Send Beckwith and Stern final bills Estimated tax payment due | **16** McCary deck repair |
| **17** 2:00-4:00— Prepare job site for Wilder job 5:00—Meeting at McGinnis insurance agency Call Wilder re: job | **18** Wilder bedroom addition all day | **19** 8:00-3:00— Wilder bedroom addition 3:30—Dentist | **20** Wilder bedroom addition all day Call Grinsay Lumber re: special shingles for Wilder job Annual pickup truck inspection due by Friday | **21** Wilder bedroom addition all day | **22** Send Wilder bill (halfway through job) Annual pickup truck inspection Cathy's birthday tomorrow—order flowers | **23** Call to thank Dr. Inverness for referring Wilder job Beckwith kitchen punchlist items Cathy's birthday |
| **24** Review all accounts and payments and pay bills | **25** Wilder bedroom addition | **26** 9:00-3:00— Wilder bedroom addition P.M.—John Batsler to begin electrical work for Wilder job today | **27** 11:00-5:00— Wilder bedroom addition A.M.—Herman Klee to begin drywall for Wilder today | **28** Open day | **29** Wilder bedroom addition all day | **30** Jewish holiday— do not disturb Mr. Wilder Carpet McCary deck (pmt. due upon completion; have bill ready) |

get yourself a month-at-a-glance-style calendar. This is one that shows one month at a time and has large boxes for each day. Keep the calendar on your desk if you have one, somewhere that's handy when you are doing your Sunday night planning for the week. When you're not in your office, take it with you.

You'll use your calendar for scheduling two types of activities: jobs and reminders/follow-ups.

**Scheduling jobs**   Since you already know how many hours of work each job takes (one of the advantages of using the hourly rate method of billing), scheduling time to do the work of each job is easy.

- Look at your calendar and pick the days or partial days to do the work.

- Where possible, do jobs from start to finish without interruption. This minimizes down time for commuting, cleaning up, preparing the site, and similar tasks.

- If you can't schedule the job on consecutive days because of factors outside your control (materials or other contractors aren't available), then the best you can do is schedule jobs for the most efficient times and stick to the schedule.

- If you find that jobs are continually taking a lot more time to do than you estimated in your contract, adjust your estimating for future jobs. There's not much that you can do about this job, but at least you can benefit from your mistakes.

Making and following a schedule saves you time—and time is money. You don't waste time running unnecessary errands, and you don't lose time waiting for materials or other contractors. But there's another value to keeping a schedule. You make a statement to your customers and to your suppliers that you are a pro-

> **Q:** **What do I put on my calendar?**
>
> **A:** - Work schedules and specific appointments
> - When to send bills every month
> - When bills are overdue and you need to follow up
> - When to pay your bills and salaries (if you have any)
> - Reminders to do small things such as send thank-you notes, announcements regarding your business, and season's greetings cards
> - The times you have set aside for handling phone calls
> - The time each week to be available to give estimates for new jobs or make repairs or adjustments to completed jobs
> - When to pick up supplies
> - When to pay yourself (remember, you need to pay yourself since you are on salary, too)
> - Important personal dates

fessional and you work in a professional manner. Contractors and material suppliers you work with regularly will quickly realize that you are a person who operates on a firm schedule and that you expect those who work with you and for you to do likewise.

When you force yourself to schedule your time, it quickly becomes very clear how much time you need to allow between and during jobs. As you know, you can use a lot of time in conversations with owners and other contractors, picking up supplies, trash disposal, and even eating lunch. When it's down in black and white, you can better see how to use your time to the best advantage so that you earn the income you want.

**Scheduling reminders**   Use your calendar as a tool to help you remember all the other important tasks associated with running your business. Throughout the next sections, I'll be talking about communicating with your customers and promoting your business. Your calendar will help you remember when to do these. Use a small portion of each daily box on your calendar for noting things that you have told someone else you will do. For example, when you tell an owner that you will phone him next week, write a note on your calendar on that day as a reminder. Or, if you are supposed to check to see if materials have arrived at a supplier by a particular date, write it down on that date.

Your calendar can help you keep track of when customers should send you money and also when you need to pay your bills. You don't have to rely on your memory, and you don't want to rely on notes scattered all over the place. Your calendar helps you to take your commitments seriously. Your time and effort will be paid back many times over in increased customer satisfaction, which means customers will pay their bills sooner and gladly recommend you to friends.

### ■ Staying in touch

Another important task to keep your business running smoothly and to help your business grow is communicating with customers, other contractors, suppliers, and so on. I'll cover two major categories (phone calls and letters) and offer some ways to spend less time doing work that isn't paying you any money—though it sure will save you money.

---

**TUESDAY 31**

7:00 Finish laying floor at
     Kenworth's house in morning
12:00 Lunch
Pick up Nelson materials at 1:00
Drop off tax records at accountant
     at 3:00
Meet with Mr. Drake to discuss new
     job at 4:30

**Reminders:**
Call Stu about working on
     Anderson job
Second payment due from Kaufmans

**Phone rules**   Your phone is a key tool for working with your customers and growing your business. At best, lost messages and unreturned phone calls mean delays in a job and, at worst, they can mean lost jobs. Because the phone is such an important tool, it's easy to forget who's in charge. Your phone works for you, not the other way around. Phones are meant to help you handle your calls in a timely, professional manner without having your work constantly interrupted. Follow these rules to stay on top of your calling:

*People don't expect an instant response, but they do expect and deserve a call back on the same day.*

1. Use the answering machine. Whenever you are not in your office, set your answering machine or answering service to take your messages. If you are working in your office on something that needs your undivided attention, it's okay to let the machine pick up your call so that you don't have to be interrupted.

2. Get your messages from your machine two or three times a day. Write down every message along with names, phone numbers, dates, and times of calls.

3. Set aside a time each day to make your routine phone calls. Ideally, this should be the same time each day. Once people get to know that this is your schedule, they will accept that this is a way to run a business smoothly. People don't expect an instant response, but they do expect and deserve a call back on the same day.

4. You can break the third rule in two different situations: When you need to let customers know about last-minute delays and when returning a call that could lead to a new customer. In the first case, if you will be late for a scheduled appointment, always call to let the customer know. Since you are building your reputation on timeliness and dependability, you can't afford to be casual about your scheduled appointments. When you call to say that you will be late, tell your customer exactly why. He probably won't be happy about the delay, but he is likely to be much more understanding if he knows the reason. In the second case—the new customer—you should make these calls a priority. When potential customers are shopping around, it's very important that they get a quick response from you.

**Don't Let the Tail Wag the Dog**

Bob, an electrician who is trying to grow his business, thought that his new cell phone was just the ticket. He carried it everywhere and gave the number out to customers, suppliers, and even family members. He wasn't going to miss an opportunity. Sounded like a good idea, but he didn't think so the other day. When he was trying to finish wiring the Claytons' addition, he was interrupted six times in three hours. Later, when he was going over his estimate for a new service panel with Sally Smith, the cell phone interrupted them three times. The Clayton job is running a day late and Sally Smith gave the job to another contractor—one whom she felt had the time to really listen to what she wanted.

5. Use a cell phone only if you can remember when to turn it on and when to turn it off. It can be very economical to make your phone calls during the day from your truck, but don't let it rule your life. You are in charge of your schedule. Be sure to turn the phone off when you are working.

**The written word** You are much too busy to spend a lot of time sending letters, but you do need to drag out the typewriter about once a week to do some important letters. I'll put in another plug here for an inexpensive computer. With a word processor, you are able to create a library of form letters and contracts to use over and over again without typing them in each time. Do you think that when your lawyer sends you a contract that she or her secretary created it just for you? Not likely.

In addition to contracts, invoices, and demand letters, there are a few more things that will help your business run smoother and grow larger.

- **CONFIRMATION:** It's always helpful to confirm in writing with subcontractors and material suppliers, particularly if you don't come in contact with them very often or if the job is scheduled far in the future. A confirmation letter eliminates any doubt or confusion.

- **THANK YOU FOR YOUR BUSINESS:** This is a simple note thanking an owner for the opportunity to do a job and telling him that you would be pleased to work for him again. All correspondence is a form of free advertising since your letterhead on a piece of stationery is much more memorable than simply hearing the name. A thank-you note after work is completed, however, is more than advertising. It marks you as a professional and as a person who cares about your customers even after the job is done and the money is paid. The owner who receives such a letter says to himself, "I want to remember this person for future needs." That's a pretty good response to something that took 30 seconds to do and cost a few cents!

- **THANK YOU FOR YOUR REFERRAL:** When someone gives your name to a friend and you get a new job, always thank the person who sent the business your way. While a phone call is certainly good, if you want to do something a little extra but very easy, write a thank-you letter. The best thank-you letter is very brief, three sentences to be precise. If you use a computer, this is one of the form letters you can keep on it. If not, a very small amount of your or your helper's time is needed to write or type it. Because this is a personal letter, handwriting is just as good as typing. Of course, when you send such a letter, you immediately accomplish two things: You impress that person with your gratitude for what he has done, and you also place your name in front of that person as a visual reminder of your business.

**Q: What form letters do I need?**

**A:** You need the following:
- Estimate
- Letter of agreement
- Thank you for your business
- Thank you for your referral
- Reminder to subcontractor
- Reminder to supplier
- Confirmation of start date with customer
- Friendly reminder
- Final demand
- Form invoice
- Letter regarding disputes

---

- **Joel T. Slate**
**HOME IMPROVEMENT CORPORATION**
P.O. Box 192
Anywhere, Virginia 00000
Phone: (123) 123-1234  Fax: (123) 123-1235
October 1, 2000

Mr. John L. Bainbridge
17000 Stowe Lane
Anywhere, Virginia 00000

Dear Mr. Bainbridge:

Thank you very much for recommending me to Harry and Janet Tuttle. I'm starting the tile work in their kitchen next Monday and expect to complete it by the end of the week.
   I hope to be seeing you soon.

Sincerely,

Joel T. Slate

**TIP**

In your thank-you letter, mention the person who received the recommendation (the new customer) and what you are doing for him.

- **PROSPECTING:** Keep a file of good referral sources and send something to each of them occasionally. Your prospect file might include people you've worked for in the past, people who have made inquiries, businesses in your community who might need your services, and any number of people who might refer work to you in the future. You want to keep your name fresh in their minds. The "out of sight, out of mind" rule applies very strongly to prospects. If a potential customer has not received something from you within recent memory, he will forget about you.

  Keep a list of your prospects in a card file or, better still, on a computer. Send everyone on the list something once or twice a year. A holiday card in December is a sure bet; include a brief personal note, if you can. Also, the cards you use should be nondenominational so that religious preference isn't an issue.

  In addition to holiday cards, there are other good occasions for mailings. If you change your business name, if you move, or if your phone number changes because of new area codes or some other reason, these are perfect occasions to send announcements. You can have a printed card prepared simply for this purpose or you can make one on your computer.

## Getting Help

At this point, you may be feeling overwhelmed with the amount of paperwork, estimating, contracts, and phone calls that are involved in running your business. There's no doubt about it—there's a lot that goes on behind the scenes to keep your business running smoothly. While the tools I talk about can simplify them, these tasks don't go away. Since they can have a significant impact on your potential income, it makes good business sense to think carefully about the best ways to do these tasks. Simply stated, you have three choices:

- Do it yourself

- Hire someone

- Ask a family member

## ■ Doing it yourself

Many contractors choose this possibility. If you use the tips and tools in this book, you can keep the paperwork efficient and manageable. There are, however, some pitfalls to this choice:

- It makes your workday longer.

- It takes away from family time or recreation.

- It reduces the number of billable hours.

## ■ Hiring help

The second alternative, hiring someone to do these things, has some obvious benefits but possibly more drawbacks. Finding the right person can be challenging, but it may be worth the look. If what you need is someone for a couple of hours a day, there are many people to consider. There are a number of people in your community who would be willing to work at an economical rate and who could also be flexible. Consider students for after-school hours, retired people, people who are free during school hours, and people who have been out of the workforce and would welcome an entry-level position.

The cost of such a person, even part time, may be more than you can support, especially when you consider the insurance and taxes that you may need to pay. On the flip side, if you can pay a person $10 per hour for five hours a week and thus free up five additional hours that you can bill out at $30 or $40 per hour, you may come out ahead, even with the taxes and insurance.

## ■ Keeping it in the family

The third alternative, using a family member where it is possible, can be a very good choice in many situations. For example, a spouse or a parent could be available during a fixed hour or two each day for phone calls, dealings with other parties, answering the needs of owners, handling materials, arranging orders and deliveries, and coordinating with subcontractors and helpers.

The other big advantage of using a person with whom you have a regular relationship is that such a person picks up your work style and can discuss each of the tasks she is doing with you. That sort of coordination can go a long way toward accomplishing the best possible relationships with suppliers, other workers, and owners. Since family members care about your work and share your goals for success, they are very motivated to make your business more profitable. This kind of team can accomplish things that are rarely achieved by paid employees.

There's another side to working with family. Not all families can do it well. While there are many success stories, there are also those stories of family tensions that arose from a family-run business. You will be the best judge of what will work in your situation.

---

### Family Ties that Work

Matt has a successful plumbing business. Actually, Matt and his wife Renee have a successful plumbing business. They have worked out a system that works for them both. Matt does all the plumbing work at the customer sites and is gone most days from 7:00 A.M. to 6:00 P.M. Renee works full time caring for their home, their two children, and is responsible for all the plumbing business and financial matters.

Every day from 1:00 P.M. to 3:00 P.M., before the kids get home from school, she does her office work. She orders and pays for supplies and all other bills, schedules jobs, handles matters related to employees, and takes care of insurance and taxes. If she can't get everything done in those two hours, she fits it in other times during the day, evening, or weekends. She handles all of the contacts with customers. If you phone Matt for a plumbing job, Renee will answer the phone or she'll shortly return the phone call left on the answering machine. Renee knows all their customers and they know that when she says something will happen, her assurance is as good as her husband's.

It's really a win-win arrangement for them. And speaking of winning, since Matt doesn't need to catch up on paperwork when he gets home, he and Renee can both go watch their son's Little League team play.

# ▬Growing Your Business

To improve your profitability, you can price your work correctly and work efficiently, but that may not be enough to meet your financial goals. To increase your annual income, you may need to expand your business. The two main sources for new work are:

- New jobs from your existing customers

- New jobs through referrals from your customers

## ■ New work from current customers

Good work, timeliness, and fair prices will go a long way toward getting you the next job from existing clients. But there are other ways, too. Use your current job as a springboard for new work. One of the surest ways to get another job from an existing client is to talk about the new job while you are working on the current one. Since you should be talking with an owner a few times during the course of the job to keep him involved, you can use these times to bring up other types of work. There are several types of so-called "add-on" work, including economy of scale, existing problems, potential problems, and new work.

- **THE ECONOMY OF SCALE APPROACH:** This approach is a natural when you are replacing a worn-out item and there are many such items in the house or office. For example, suppose you are an electrician replacing a ceiling lighting fixture that has broken. When you show the owner the proposed replacement, consider saying, "I don't know if you've ever given any thought to replacing all of these, but when I was in the ceiling I could see that the others are not far behind this one." Many owners will then ask what it would cost to replace all of the ceiling fixtures. At that point, the economy of scale approach becomes very natural: "I'll have to check it out, but if you do them all at once I think that it will run something in the neighborhood of $70 per fixture." Such a statement after you have quoted the owner a price of $95 for the single fixture virtually seals the deal.

- **THE EXISTING PROBLEM APPROACH:** This is also known as the "I noticed the problem you are having with your (___)

when I was walking through the house" approach. It depends upon your knowing a way to fix an obvious problem or to make a substantial improvement in something you can see the owner is currently using. An example is a cabinet or shelf where a repair such as a hinge or knob has been jury-rigged or a counter where the laminate is beginning to come loose. You can tell as soon as you mention it whether or not the owner has been thinking about it from time to time. If he has, he will probably ask you about the cost of reworking all of the cabinets or relaminating the counter. If he has not, he may or may not give thought to the matter, but you have lost nothing by mentioning it.

- **THE POTENTIAL PROBLEM APPROACH:** This approach is usually appropriate when you notice a defect that will surely cause an owner difficulty in the future or a defect that presents a hazard. A common example is where a plumber is asked to

## Making Your Own Opportunities

People without electricity for days often have trouble with their electrical appliances when current is resumed. This is a good opportunity not only to fix the problem that the customer called about but also to sell something that could help prevent the problem in the future. A savvy electrician will do his homework about home generators before making such calls. He might print out information about home generators, emphasizing their ability to start automatically when power is disrupted and the versatility of power sources for them.

To someone who has been without electric power for days (even better, someone who has also been without water because they are on a well), the simple question "Did you ever consider a home generator?" is a little like asking someone who has just walked across the Mojave Desert if he has ever considered a cold drink. It's no surprise that electricians find that people in reasonably expensive homes who lose electricity for days often ask, "What would be involved?" A properly prepared electrician takes it from there. If he succeeds, he has almost surely sold a new job where he can earn the markup on a $5,000 to $7,000 12-kilowatt generator and the profit on installation services of about the same value. Not a bad deal for a discussion that takes less than 15 minutes.

fix an appliance such as a sink or toilet and when he turns off the water, he realizes that the pipes leading to the bathroom or kitchen are badly decayed. This is the sort of thing that a conscientious contractor always brings to an owner's attention. Another example is an electrician who is replacing a bathroom ceiling fan. While in the bathroom, he notices an outlet that is within reach of the bathtub. This is a clear violation of all building codes and a life-threatening situation. A conscientious electrician should mention it to the owner.

- **NEW WORK OR PRODUCT:**   This approach suggests the possibility of doing something entirely new for the owner. Often the new work is a spinoff of the original job that you were working on. Perhaps there is some piece of equipment that you could sell to the owner that would prevent the situation that you just fixed (see the example of the enterprising electrician and the power generators in the sidebar on the facing page).

You may feel awkward and pushy having conversations like these with owners. That's not surprising, since some people are more comfortable than others with promoting their services. For some contractors, any kind of conversation is difficult. They'd rather just do the work and not talk about it. But it's like any new skill: The more that you do it, the better you will become. If you thoughtfully and honestly offer your customers one of the suggestions mentioned above—without being overly aggressive—you will find that most will be appreciative. You are simply pointing out possibilities that will in the long run save them money, ensure their safety, or both. This will result in new jobs from owners for whom you are working and will assure you of longer and more satisfying relationships with your customers.

## New jobs through referrals

Where do you get new customers? Do people look you up in the yellow pages? How about ads in your local newspaper? The fact is, most small contractors get new business by word-of-mouth recommendations. It is very important to get as many personal recommendations as possible. Here are a few tips to help increase your number of referrals.

- **DO GOOD WORK**:   Once you are done with a job, your work speaks for you and so do your customers. If they were satis-

*Most small contractors get new business by word-of-mouth recommendations.*

**Who Should You Tell about Your Business?**
- Material suppliers
- Clients for whom you have already done work
- Contractors you know in your trade
- Contractors in other trades
- General contractors
- Construction managers
- Insurance companies
- Lawyers
- Accountants
- Friends, family, neighbors

fied with the work, if the job was finished on time, and if the job looks great, most owners can't help but spread the word. And when people see your work, they ask the owner who did it and if he was happy working with you.

Joel T. Slate

# Home Improvement Corporation

P.O. Box 192

Anywhere, Virginia 00000

**PHONE: (123) 123-1234  FAX: (123) 123-1235**
**E-mail: jslate@xxx.net**

Tile – Slate – Stone Work – Grout and Tile Repairs
*Call for free estimates*

- **SPREAD THE WORD:** Sometimes the most obvious suggestions are the ones that we think about last. Don't assume that people know that you would like new work. You need to tell them. There is no downside to letting someone know about your business and that you are willing to talk to new customers. Just be sure that you don't come across as so desperate that people wonder about the quality of your work. Simple statements such as "Could I give you my business card in case you or someone you know could ever use my services?" or "Please give me a call if I can ever help you" are enough to make your message clear. Be sure that you have a supply of business cards handy at all times and don't be shy about giving them out.

- **SAY THANK YOU:** Thank each person who refers business to you every time he does so. This is often overlooked, so don't make that mistake. Saying "thank you" is not only a deserved courtesy, but it is very good business. In a surprising number of situations, you'll get a second or a third referral from the same person. Your call or note will bring your name to mind again. Most referrals are made rather quickly, and the person on someone's mind is the one most likely to get the business.

- **STAY IN TOUCH:** Keep your name fresh in people's minds. The section on "The Written Word" (see pp. 56–58) covers keeping a list of prospects and sending them holiday cards, change of address notices, and so on. These are very important tools for growing your business.

The tools in this chapter may not seem difficult to use and they aren't. The challenge is that it might seem that using calendars, writing letters, and spending time on tasks that pay you nothing is a tremendous waste of your valuable time. Don't believe that for a minute.

Your question cannot be "Should I use these tools?" but rather "How can I use them in the shortest possible time?" and "What do I have to gain?"

The answer to the first question is *practice.* The more you work at scheduling your time and really sticking to it, the easier it becomes. The same is true for writing things down on your calendar and remembering to look at it. If you are able to get some help, paid or otherwise, that's a bonus.

The answer to the second question is that contractors who do these things make a lot more money than those who do not. If you doubt this, ask five to ten contractors who are willing to tell you their income whether they do these things or not. You will find that those who make the most money are the ones who are taking the time to make their businesses run well and to grow new business. They are using these tools every day because their businesses and their incomes depend upon it. It's up to you whether you want to use any or all of these business tools, but you can be sure that your decision will show in your bank account.

---

### Business Card Dos and Don'ts

- Keep it simple.
- Put your company name, address, phone, fax, and e-mail on it.
- Tell what you do on your card. Make sure that people know what your trade is.
- Have your local quick printer make you a simple but clear card.
- Keep a supply of business cards with you always.
- Use a standard business card.
- Don't try to say too much on your card.
- Don't pay a lot of money to a graphic designer for a fancy card.
- Don't use a Rolodex card.

---

### Simple Ways to Get New Business

- Suggest new or similar work to current customers.
- Tell current customers about any repairs or safety hazards you see.
- Thank customers for their work, preferably in writing.
- Keep a list of referral sources, including your past and current customers, and send them holiday cards or other announcements.
- Return phone calls promptly, even when they do not concern a new job.
- Give estimates on a timely basis.
- Be available for questions, repairs, and adjustments of work you have done.

# CHAPTER 4

# Managing the Paper Chase

**M**oney comes in and money goes out. That's just the normal flow of life, whether it's your business life or your personal life. Chapter 1 covered ways to make sure that your job is priced so that your hard work earns you the most money possible. You learned that you need to carefully track all of your expenses to decide if they are general overhead expenses or variable expenses. Chapter 1 covered billing and collecting payments. Now it's time to learn how to manage the paperwork in the easiest and most efficient ways. This includes learning:

- Why managing your paperwork is important

- What a record is

- How to track money in vs. money out (payments vs. expenses)

- What records to keep

- Where and how to keep them

- Ways to correctly use your records

*"I don't have time to be playing around with all kinds of papers. I have work to do to earn my living," one contractor told me.*

## ▰Getting Motivated

Many contractors believe that keeping records is just too much work in light of all of their other responsibilities. "I don't have time to be playing around with all kinds of papers. I have work to do to earn my living," one contractor told me. While this is certainly an honest and typical response, my contractor friend is off track for two very important reasons. First, if you set up a good system for managing your paperwork (called *record keeping*) and use it on a regular basis, the amount of time needed to keep it up is extremely small. Second, like it or not, record keeping *is* part of your work. It's part of what you need to do to earn a living. It does no good to get profitable jobs if you don't follow through and handle the expenses and payments correctly. Accurate record keeping makes sure that you:

- Pass along all the right expenses to your customers

- Know exactly how much you spend in general overhead expenses and thus charge an adequate hourly rate

### How to Have Uncle Sam Pay You for 25 Hours

If you keep track of your expenses and claim all of the deductions that you're entitled to, it's almost like having the IRS pay you without working the extra hours. Let's look at an example of using the home office deduction.

Although you'll have to discuss your specific circumstances with your accountant, home-office deductions are generally available to people who have no other office and who have a small portion of their house devoted exclusively to their business. In general, home-office deductions are available for a proportion of the expenses of your house that's equal to the proportion of your house's square footage that's used by the home office. If you have a 2,000-sq.-ft. house and use 200 sq. ft. of it exclusively for your office, you'll be entitled to deduct from your income 10% of the expenses related to your house, such as insurance, gas, electricity, and mortgage interest.

Suppose that all expenses related to your house come to $20,000 per year. If you qualified for a home-office deduction, you would have a $2,000 deduction from your gross income for both federal and state tax purposes. If you pay approximately 25% of your income in federal and state taxes, these deductions would be worth $500 per year. Add to this the specific expenses of a home office that are completely deductible, such as a business phone, fax, stationery, and so forth, and the whole package related to your home office is probably worth in the neighborhood of $1,000. If you charge $40 per hour for your work, that deduction earns you the same as working 25 hours. It's almost as though Uncle Sam is paying you for keeping good records!

- Apply payments from customers correctly

- Know which customers have paid you and which have not, so that you can follow up with the "have nots" in time

- Have all the records that you need so that you can enjoy the greatest tax benefit

- Be ready at all times for any situations where you need to prove your expenses, such as insurance claims or requests by customers

## What Is a Record?

Let's start with the basics: What is a record? A record is anything that shows how you spent money or how you earned money. This includes such things as the invoices that you send to your customers, the receipts for supplies that you buy, credit card receipts when you buy gas, even receipts that you get when you buy small items for cash. Big or little, they are all important.

There are two types of records that you'll be tracking:

- Money in—customer payments

- Money out—expenses

### Customer payments

Tracking customer payments is important for two reasons:

- To know which customers still owe you money so that you can follow up with them

- To ensure that the money you receive gets deposited into your bank account

After all of the effort that you put into the contract and the job, you want to be sure that you know precisely how much you have been paid by each customer. You can't follow up on late payments, as described in chapter 1, unless you know who has paid and how much. In the filing system that I will cover, you will have a separate folder for each customer or job with all of the customer's expense records and your bills. When you get a payment from a customer, you can simply note the amount of the payment, the check number, and the date of that payment on your copy of the bill.

When you record a payment in your checkbook, note the customer's name so you know where the payment came from. In those cases where you are depositing a number of payments from different customers at the same time, you should mark the deposit slip to identify each customer's payment. Of course, you should keep all deposit slips in your banking records. When a customer makes a final payment, make a note in that customer's file that the account has been paid in full.

You want to be able to follow up with those customers who are late. If you followed the steps in chapter 1, you made a note of which payments were due and when right on your calendar. If you have only a few jobs open at one time, this system is probably all that you need. When the customer pays, in addition to making a note on the bill in his folder, cross the note off your calendar. If you have a large number of jobs open at the same time, you may want to consider a computerized program to organize your billing. There are a number of good but simple accounting software programs that will help you manage your accounts receivable.

Be sure to keep your records of payments from each customer and your banking records up to date. You'll need these to keep track of who paid the money you are owed to prepare your tax materials for your accountant each year.

## ■ Expenses

Keeping track of your expenses is not difficult, but there are a few rules to follow:

- **NEVER MIX BUSINESS AND PERSONAL FINANCES:** Pay all business expenses from a separate business account. Do not mix business expenses with personal expenses for you and your family (see pp. 89–92).

- **KEEP ALL RECEIPTS:** This is also necessary for tax purposes, which will be discussed later in this book.

- **SWEAT THE SMALL STUFF:** Pay every expense, however small, whether you paid it with a credit card, a check, or cash,

> **Sweat the Small Stuff**
> It's a mistake to think that overlooking a few small expenses will not make any difference in your income. Two or three dollars of overlooked expenses a day are equivalent to $1,000 in expenditures per year. Since expenses are completely deductible from income for tax purposes, the annual loss is significant. If you want to really increase the profitability of your business, take each of the small steps described in this book. Together they will increase your income by thousands of dollars per year.

from your business account. Make no exceptions! Some contractors pay for small expenses with their own cash and often lose the receipts. Cash for small expenses, known as *petty cash*, should come from the business account as well. Keep receipts for cash purchases as carefully as all other receipts. If expenses and cash for small expenses are always paid from the same account, there will be a continuous record of the payment of expenses and nothing will be lost.

---

### What about Replacement Items?

How do you handle replacement items such as drill bits and sandpaper? Are they general overhead or are they expenses of particular jobs? If possible, charge replacement items to a particular job. It's best to keep your general overhead as low as possible. Remember, you will use general overhead in figuring your hourly rate, so if overhead is high, your hourly rate will also be high.

---

**General overhead vs. variable expenses** Once you've established a method for keeping track of expenses, you need a method for deciding whether each expense is general overhead or variable. Remember that general overhead expenses are those that are involved in running your business and are not related to one specific job, whereas variable expenses are related to just one job.

Chapter 1 covered general overhead vs. variable expenses in relation to pricing your work, so you know that tracking expenses is important for that. In addition, to get the greatest tax benefit from your expenses, you must have complete records of what you spent.

On p. 11, there is a checklist that tells you which expenses are general overhead. This checklist covers most areas. However, there are certain expenses that may be treated as general overhead expenses or expenses relating to a particular job, depending upon the contractor's preference. For example, gas that you buy for your pickup truck during a job that requires a lot of driving may be categorized as either general or variable. Another example is when you need to replace tools during certain jobs, such as when sawblades are destroyed by using them for cutting that is necessary for that job. Drill bits, sandpaper, and other items may also be exhausted in a particular job.

It's generally better to assign these expenses to a specific job and not to general overhead. You want to keep the general overhead portion of expenses as low as possible so that it won't unduly raise the hourly rate that you have set. It's also easier to tell whether a job is profitable when you have a complete list of the expenses for that job.

# What Records to Keep and How to Keep Them

The first thing you must do to keep good records is decide what records you need to keep. Do this before the start of each tax year. If you don't do this in advance of each year, you'll never do it. Once papers start piling up, it is almost impossible to organize.

## ■ First things first—make a list

How do you know what records you need to keep? There are a number of sources to use:

- **TALK TO YOUR ACCOUNTANT:** While not mandatory, a good place to start is a talk with your accountant. He can explain to you quickly exactly what records you need for each tax deduction to which you're entitled. These will most likely include all of your general overhead expenses as well as all records related to your income. For example, your accountant will prob-

---

**Q:** **What records should I keep?**

**A:** Check with your accountant or the IRS about your particular situation, but here's a general list of records you should keep:

**Income:**
- Sales to customers
- Interest income
- Other income

**Expenses:**
- Legal and professional fees, such as accountants and lawyers
- Bank charges
- Postage
- Office supplies
- Dues and subscriptions
- Advertising
- Truck expenses
- Phone line/fax line
- Printing

- Work materials (general overhead)
- Work materials (specific jobs)
- Freight charges
- Taxes
- Wages
- Property insurance
- Workers' compensation
- Medical insurance
- Liability insurance
- Unemployment insurance
- Utilities
- Interest payments on loans
- Tools and equipment

## Twelve Steps to Good Record Keeping

1. Start before your business year begins.
2. Talk to your accountant about what records are needed for taxes.
3. Put together a complete list of all types of records needed, tax and otherwise.
4. Make a folder for each type of record.
5. Make a folder for each job. If you have more than one job for a customer, make a separate folder for each, but keep the folders together.
6. Make a folder for each special matter such as insurance claims.
7. Make a box for each business year.
8. Organize the folders in the boxes in the order that makes the most sense to you.
9. Put a note on each record (receipt) to show what it was for.
10. Put each record in the correct folder daily.
11. If a record applies to two or more folders, such as a receipt for supplies for several jobs, make copies of that record for each folder.
12. Always keep the original copies of your records. If you need to give someone a record, give him a photocopy.

ably tell you that expenses related to your pickup truck are deductible, and you will need to keep those receipts. These generally include insurance, gas and oil, repairs, replacements of tires, and so forth. Likewise, you need copies of all invoices or bills that you send to your customers. Depending upon your particular trade and any special aspects of your tax situation that your accountant will explain, there may be other tax deductions available to you.

■ **FIND OUT ABOUT TRADE-RELATED REQUIREMENTS:** Consider whether there are records that are of particular concern to your trade. For example, in some trades there are record-keeping requirements concerning licenses. In every trade there are particular insurance requirements, but these vary depending upon whether you're a general contractor and other matters. Talk with other contractors in your trade. They may think of areas that you've overlooked.

■ **COMPILE A LIST OF ALL OF YOUR CURRENT JOBS AND CUSTOMERS:** You will need to keep records for each of them.

Make a checklist of all of the items that you have found from your accountant, your trade or other requirements, and your current jobs. This is your total list of records that you need to keep. Don't worry about the length of the list; it doesn't matter as long as you have included every item. Don't skip items because they seem to be small or even because you don't know if you'll have every item every year. Be as thorough as you can, but if you overlook some category, you can add it later.

Don't take these tasks lightly because they relate to taxes (which few people enjoy thinking about) or because they require some of your time. The difference between doing these things the right way or the wrong way can be a difference of thousands of dollars of income to you each year.

Your first list will probably take you some time to do, but take heart, you don't need to do it all over each year. There may be slight changes in what records you need to keep each year because of changes in tax laws or changes related to your particular trade or licenses and so forth. But, thank goodness, these will be very few and far between. Once you have your basic list of the necessary records, that list will serve you for many years.

## ■ Keeping your records organized

Once you've figured out the list of records that you need to keep, the next step is to come up with a method for keeping those records without significant time or expense. Many contractors simply throw all of their receipts and bills in a box or drawer, with the thought that they'll straighten them out later. "I don't have time to spend on this sort of thing on a daily basis" is a remark I've heard many times. Staying organized takes only seconds more than it takes to throw a piece of paper in a box or drawer. When you come home after a 10-hour to 12-hour work-day, the last thing you want to do is fuss with the papers you've accumulated during the day. I'll talk about a very simple system, but you could also keep track of all of these records on your computer, if you wish.

> **Every Hit Counts**
> Smart business is not just about home runs. It's also about a lot of singles, doubles, and triples. Each of the tools you'll learn about in this book makes a contribution to your improved financial situation, some large and some small. But just as it takes hits as well as homers to win a ball game, each of these tools is an important part of your winning financial picture.

> **Computer Record Keeping**
> If you have a computer, you can use it to help you keep track of your income and expenses. There are some very good accounting software programs that are easy to use and help you prepare your invoices, manage customer payments, and put all of your records into a form that is easy for your accountant to use when he prepares your taxes. If you use a computer, however, you still need to keep the paper copies of all of your receipts! You can't throw them out once you have put the information on your computer.

**Minimum requirements**  The best method for keeping records begins with two key items—a few cardboard file boxes and a box or two of manila folders.

- **FILE BOXES:** Often referred to as banker's boxes, these cardboard cartons hold either standard-size or legal-size folders, depending upon which way you use them, and have lids and handgrips on each side. You won't need very many of them, but you must use one or more for each business year. Keep each business year in a separate box. Of course, you could use a standard file cabinet if you'd like, but these boxes will work just fine.

- **MANILA FOLDERS:** It's up to you whether to use standard-size or legal-size folders. Legal-size folders are a bit more expensive, so go with the standard unless you have long documents to keep, such as building plans.

**Set up in three simple steps** Once you have your list, your file boxes, and your manila folders, it should take you or your helper no more than an hour to set up your filing system. There are just three simple steps:

1. Put together the boxes, which should take about two minutes.

2. Make a separate folder for each item on your list. Depending upon how many different categories you have, this shouldn't take more than 10 to 15 minutes. Write on the tab of each folder what it's for. For example, write "Gas and Oil for Pickup Truck" or "New and Replacement Tools." Write "Business Phone Expenses" on a folder for bills for your business phone and any cellular phones or pagers you might use.

3. Organize your folders in a way that makes sense to you so that you can find them easily. You may want to organize them in straight alphabetical order, or you may want to group them by the kind of expense. For example, put the folders for expenses related to your truck one after another in the file box. The same is true for folders related to your home office and for folders related to general overhead, insurance, and so on. If you have more than one job for each customer, make a separate folder for each job and keep all of the jobs for the same customer together.

---

**Q: Do I need to spend a lot of time on record keeping?**

**A:** No. Making a system you'll use for the entire year will take you less than one day. Keeping that system complete, up to date, and workable for all of your needs won't take more than a few minutes a day.

Unless you're a very unusual contractor, you'll need only one file box each work year. If not, you can simply move some of the manila folders to another box during the year. Be sure to label each file box for each year, something like "Business records for 2001." Keep them in a safe place where there's no chance that they'll be thrown away by mistake.

---

### Record Keeping in the Trenches

Hank is a tile installer and very good at what he does. Unfortunately, the constant kneeling to do floor work, even with protectors, is starting to take its toll on Hank's 45-year-old knees. Hank isn't certain whether his physical difficulties will ultimately have workers' compensation or unemployment insurance consequences, but he knows enough to keep the necessary records. Hank set up a filing system like the one described in this chapter. Here's how he makes it work for him.

On a typical day, Hank buys gas for his truck, gets tile and grout for two of his jobs, and buys two small replacement tools. When he arrives home, he spends a few minutes in his office. On his desk are several business bills, including a phone bill and a bill for the semiannual pickup truck insurance. There is also a package of fax paper he ordered by phone with a receipt. In this day, he has accumulated six receipts that he needs to take care of. Here's what Hank does:

- He files the receipts for the gas, tools, and fax paper in the proper manila folders.
- He puts the phone bill and the insurance bill on his desk to pay when he normally pays all of his bills (Sunday night). After that, he'll put the receipts in the correct folders.
- The receipt for tile and grout applies to two jobs, but it's only one piece of paper. Hank writes in the margin of the receipt next to each item which of the two jobs it applies to. He runs off a copy on his fax machine and places a copy in the folders for each of the two jobs.

Hank has finished his record keeping for the day, and it has taken him less than five minutes. He does this every day for every receipt, even records that he may not need, such as doctor bills for his knees. He will be prepared for tax returns, insurance claims, and customer questions.

■ The five-minute filer

Your file box and folders are the center of your record-keeping procedures for the entire year. Getting the records into the right folder is the next step. Sounds pretty easy, which it is, but it's also important that you take just a minute to do it right. A few things to remember:

1. Always get a receipt—no matter how small the expense— whether cash, check, or charge.

2. Write on the receipt what it was for. Do it right away. The longer you wait, the easier it is to forget what you were sure you couldn't forget. It doesn't need to be a long explanation. "Nails and screws for Smith house" or "paper clips and tape for office" will do. A receipt that doesn't say what it's for is worthless, so you need to do this every time.

3. If the receipt is for materials for a particular job (a variable expense), make sure you put the name of the job on the receipt. You will file this in the job file so that you can bill it to your customer.

4. If you are paying by check, write in your check ledger exactly what the check is for.

5. If you are buying materials that fall into two different folder categories, mark on the receipt what each item was for and make a copy of the receipt for each different folder. For example, if you stopped at the building-supply store and got 2x4s for one job and kitchen cabinets for another, mark the name of the job next to each item. When you get back to your office, make a copy of the receipt and put copies in both folders.

6. Take time each day to file your receipts in their folders. You're looking at adding two minutes to the end of your 10-hour day, but these two minutes will save you big money. If you have someone helping you with the office work, this can be part of her job.

If you make a visit to your "command central" file box a part of your daily routine, you'll save valuable time running your office and significant tax benefits. You can't afford the time to do it any other way. Take a look at Hank's story in the sidebar on p. 75 to see how a real contractor can work the paperwork into a busy day. Hank's method is bulletproof. It will work for any contractor in any trade. But don't allow days to go by without filing the records. When you do, you may find that you have forgotten to write the purpose on some cash or credit card receipts and that you haven't divided records such as Hank's tile and grout receipt. If you do what Hank does on a daily basis, you'll catch these oversights when you file the records because you won't have to think back over more than the day you have just finished.

## When It's Time to Use the Records

During the course of a year, you may need to use the records that you've kept. Since you've set up your system carefully and filed all of your records, it will be easy to get information when you need it. There are several typical times when you'll need to use your records:

- **BILLING YOUR CUSTOMER:** This filing method is a real bonus when it comes time to bill your job. Since you put all of your receipts in the folder for that job, you simply pull out the job folder to see what's there. You can easily make copies to

---

### Worth Your Time?

Alice was one of those contractors who cried, "I don't have time for paperwork and filing." She knew where everything was in her office, or so she claimed until the day when she was preparing the bill for Mr. Cooper's new kitchen. This was an expensive job with very elaborate cabinets. Alice couldn't find the bill for the cabinets but remembered exactly how much they cost because they were so expensive. She submitted her bill without a copy of the receipt.

It seems that Mr. Cooper's memory wasn't as good as Alice's. He refused to pay such an exorbitant bill without some proof. Two phone calls with Mr. Cooper and three phone calls and two trips to the cabinetmaker is what it took to get a duplicate receipt. It took Alice the better part of a day (seven hours at $40 per hour). Mr. Cooper has decided not to have Alice do the basement remodeling job that he was thinking about. She didn't seem too professional to him, and he certainly didn't recommend her to any of his friends after that. So how much was her time worth?

attach to the bill. Keeping track of expenses may seem like a simple thing, but if you don't do it right, you're throwing money away.

Even when a job is set at a fixed price for all work and materials, it's important to know what expenses were actually paid so that you'll know for the future whether the job was profitable. If you correctly use the hourly-rate method to price a job and you anticipate and properly bill all necessary materials and other expenses, the job should be a profitable one.

- **TAX PREPARATION:** The most important person you need to make records available to is your accountant. Most contractors do this once a year shortly after the end of each year and hopefully well in advance of the tax filing deadline of April 15. You may need to do this more often if you have to make quarterly or other tax payments. Some accountants want to review all of the records, and others just need a summary in each category. Since you are paying for your accountant's time in either case, you should always provide him with a total in each category. You can do this easily by adding up the expenses in each folder once a year, even though this may not be your favorite annual task. If you have office help, the helper can handle this for you. If you are using a computer accounting program, it will give you these totals almost automatically.

- **INSURANCE CLAIMS:** Insurance companies will need copies of records when you have a claim.

It doesn't matter who is getting the records or for what purpose. Your system is complete and up to date at all times.

## ■ Playing it safe when sharing your records

There are three important safeguards you should use when you need to share your records.

- **MAKE COPIES:** With the possible exception of your accountant with whom you'll work out a special system, you should never give your only copy of any record to anyone. Always make a copy of the record and keep the original in the folder.

Many people don't return copies of records even when they're asked to do so. Even if they do, you may need to use the record for something else while it's being used.

- **GIVE THEM ONLY WHAT THEY NEED:** When someone such as a customer has a legitimate reason to see your records, give him copies of all of the records necessary for the particular purpose, but no others.

- **ATTACH A LETTER OF EXPLANATION:** Briefly explain to the other party what records you're giving him and why. Keep a copy of that letter in the appropriate folder so that you'll always be able to show what you did. An insurance claim is a perfect example (see Jake Journeyman's story and letter on pp. 80–81). Jake would then put a copy of the letter in a new folder labeled something like "Insurance claim for pickup truck robbery of January 12, 2001."

Since the records that you'd be sending to your insurance company are clear from the letter and since you have the originals in your folders, it's not necessary to make another set of copies to go with your file copy of the letter. On the other hand, it doesn't take much extra time to make another copy of those records and attach them to your copy of the letter. What is important is that you have a full record of the insurance claim you've made and you've provided all of the needed information to your insurance agent. And you have been able to do this quickly, with no wasted time. Now your insurance company can process the claim right away and get your check out to you. You'll be amazed how easy it is if you follow these simple steps.

---

**Q:** **What should I do when someone asks for my records?**

**A:** Three things:

1. Decide what that person needs and give him copies of those records but nothing more.
2. Always keep the originals of all records, except when you have a special system worked out with your accountant.
3. Write a brief letter to the other person telling what records you're giving him and why. Keep a copy of that letter so that you have a record of what you did.

**Insurance Claims**

Suppose one day someone breaks into Jake Journeyman's truck at a job site and steals his supplies, his stereo, and some tools. Jake will have an insurance claim to deal with. You can bet that the insurance company will require proof that each item was in the truck when Jake was robbed and it will try to give each item the lowest possible value. The records that Jake has kept will help him make sure that his claim is paid fairly.

Jake's folders include records of the purchases of the supplies and tools. Since the tools were pretty new, his records will show that. Because the stereo came with the truck, Jake doesn't have a separate record, but the dealer will give him a replacement cost estimate. By having all of the records, it'll be easy for Jake to give the insurance company the information that it needs.

Jake will make a copy of each of the records. He'll double-check to make sure he didn't miss any because that would only slow up his claim. When he sends the records to his insurance agent, Jake's letter will sound like the one shown on the facing page.

*Perhaps more than any other tool, good record keeping will start to pay you back almost immediately.*

# Getting Help with Record Keeping

As mentioned in chapter 3, you may choose to get help with the office duties (including record keeping) that are required to make your business run smoothly. The record-keeping activities such as filing, preparing totals for your accountant, making copies, and writing letters of explanation are well suited to someone who is involved part time. It's an added benefit, too, to have another set of eyes review the records. Your helper can look at what you are trying to do from an outsider's point of view, which can be very helpful when questions come up.

New tools, simple tools, but as with all the other tools in this book, they will help you work smarter and save money. Perhaps more than any other tool, good record keeping will start to pay you back almost immediately. You are sure to ask, "How much more money will I make if I do these things?" Of course, this will differ from contractor to contractor. But one thing is certain: If you don't benefit by thousands of dollars a year, you'll be the only contractor I've ever met who doesn't.

The money you'll save in claiming extra tax deductions, in reducing accounting fees, in resolving insurance claims quickly and profitably, and in many other large and small matters will repay your efforts many times over. The IRS, insurance companies, and even your customers will give you all the deductions, benefits, and expenses that you are entitled to, but you do need to prove it to them with well-documented records. It's up to you to do what's necessary to get all of the financial benefits you're entitled to from your work. The steps outlined in this chapter will go a long way toward making that possible.

---

■ **XYZ Construction**

P.O. Box 123
Lexington, Kentucky 0000
Phone: (777) 333-9090  Fax: (777) 333-9091
January 20, 2001

---

ABC Insurance Company
Attn: Ms. Smith, Claim Representative
21 Pleasant Street
Cooperation, Kentucky 00000

RE: Policy # 123-345-9999

Dear Ms. Smith:

As I told you by phone on January 19, 2001, my pickup truck was robbed at a job site on January 17, 2001. The job site was at 1631 Apple Way, here in Lexington, Kentucky. The items taken from the pickup truck were:
1. The stereo
2. Tiles and grout I had purchased for the job
3. Two small tools

I am enclosing copies of my receipts for the tiles and grout and tools and a copy of the Ford dealer's estimate of the replacement cost of the stereo, which came with the pickup truck.

Please let me know if you need any further information. Thank you for your prompt attention.

Jake Journeyman
XYZ Construction

# CHAPTER 5

# Drawing the Line:
## Business vs. Personal Finances

*Contractors who treat their businesses as separate from their personal and family affairs make more money and avoid unnecessary difficulties.*

**W**hen you run your own business—particularly if you run it from your own home—the boundaries between your work life and your personal life often begin to blur. When I discuss this issue with contractors, they often say, "There's no difference between my business and personal finances" or "My work basically takes up my whole life, so why should I separate it from everything else?" While this might make sense from the point of view of someone who spends 10 hours a day, six days a week on his trade, it doesn't make sense from a business standpoint.

To the contrary, it is very important to keep your business finances and your personal finances separate. This is just as true if you're using a formal type of business such as a corporation or simply working in your own name as a sole proprietorship. Contractors who treat their businesses as separate from their personal and family affairs make more money and avoid unnecessary difficulties. As with other record keeping, make your plan for this before your business year begins. The steps outlined later in this chapter tell you what you need to do and make it as easy as possible.

While there are legal and tax reasons that require you to keep your records separate and clear, it is also something that just makes good business sense. This chapter covers three areas involved in separating business and personal finances:

- Legal and tax issues

- Practical issues dealing with making sound business choices

- How-to steps to help you keep your personal and business finances separate

## Legal Reasons for Separating Business and Personal Finances

There are several legal reasons for separating business finances from your personal finances, including compliance with tax laws, meeting the legal requirements of your contracts, and determining a value for your business. Let's start by looking at the tax issues.

**Q:** As long as I follow the tax laws, what difference does it make if I use one bank account for business and personal purposes?

**A:** If you don't keep your business finances separate from your personal finances, you won't be able to:

- Take full advantage of the tax laws
- Identify all of your business expenses
- Accurately value your business
- Decide if running your own business is better than working for someone else
- Decide if it makes sense to join forces with a partner
- Make an educated decision about hiring an employee
- Think realistically about possibilities for your retirement
- Make the best decisions about new equipment

### ■ Tax laws

As mentioned in the record-keeping discussion in chapter 4, there are many expenses that are deductible from your taxable income. But the tax laws are quite strict about what may be deducted as a business expense. As a general rule, you may deduct those things that are "necessary and reasonable" to run your business. There are two major types of deductions: expenses and capital purchases.

Most of the deductions available to the typical contractor are the expenses involved in running your business. Expenses may be deducted 100% from your gross income in a particular year. Thus, you don't pay taxes on money that is deductible as an expense. The other form of deduction is for capital purchases. Capital purchases are fairly substantial items (such as your truck or a major piece of equipment in your shop) that are considered to be an asset of your business for a number of years. Your accountant or the IRS can tell you which of your purchases are capital purchases and which are expenses.

Unless you file your own tax return, this is all that you need to know. Your job here, and the point of this chapter, is to be certain that the information you supply to your accountant is complete,

**Planning Ahead**

As with many of the recommendations in this book, you'll find the task of separating business and personal finances far easier if you plan the system you will use in advance of each year and stick to it. You don't want to be thinking of ways to do this while you're working on difficult and profitable jobs for customers. As with the record-keeping matters discussed in chapter 4, you'll find that a carefully planned system will meet your needs year after year and that you will need only to make an occasional minor change.

*If you throw all of your money and all of your bills into one big pot, it's nearly impossible to figure out what goes where.*

clear, and useful. Your accountant needs to know which of your purchases were involved in your business. If you throw all of your money and all of your bills into one big pot, it's nearly impossible to figure out what goes where.

If you spend money on something that has a business purpose and also a nonbusiness purpose, your accountant will need to divide that cost between the business and nonbusiness portion. If you keep those expenses separate, you'll not only save a good deal of your accountant's time (which means a lower bill from him), but you'll also be sure to get every possible deduction (which means you pay less tax). On the flip side, if you don't keep your business and personal finances separate, you not only risk losing some tax advantages, but you also could face difficulties with the IRS or state taxing authorities.

## ■ Contracts with customers

Your billings to your customers are based on a fixed hourly rate that you computed including your overhead expenses. If you don't track your business expenses separately from your personal expenses, the numbers that you use to compute that rate may be wrong. Once you have entered into a contract with a customer, your rate is fixed. So, if you got it wrong to begin with and later discover an overhead expense that was buried in your personal account, you'll be out of luck and, worse, out of money.

Along this same line is the possibility of overlooked charges that you should have billed directly to your customer. These may range from small items such as nails or glue to larger items such as disposal fees for wastes. A contractor may, for example, use the same landscape service to mow his lawns at home and also to do small jobs such as shrub removal at work sites. He doesn't get regular billings from the landscape contractor. In fact, the landscaper may be just the kid next door, and the contractor will pay him out of pocket. "It's just a few dollars," the contractor may say. "No big deal." As months go by, these charges add up, but the contractor can't charge them as job expenses because by the time he recognizes the expense, it's too late to pass it along to the customer. When you do this, it's like giving your money to your customers.

You Snooze, You Lose

Suzanne was willing to follow most of my advice, but the thought of two credit cards was more than she could handle. So when she was getting started in her interior painting and decorating business, she figured out what her hourly rate needed to be and landed her first big contract to do stenciling in four rooms for Janet Wilcox. Janet was pleased with the price that Suzanne put into the contract and so was Suzanne, until her credit card bill came in that month. She had bought all of her stencils, paints, brushes, sample books, and several ladders with her personal credit card and totally overlooked these expenses when she figured her hourly rate and drew up the contract. If these expenses had been kept separately, she would have been much less likely to overlook them and would have made more money on Janet's job.

If you don't separate business and personal finances carefully, you'll also have much more trouble resolving legal disputes with customers. If you're involved in a legal dispute, there is nothing more convincing than a carefully maintained record of the time you have spent on a job and the expenses you have incurred. I have found that more than half of all disputes between contractors and customers are resolved when a contractor sends the customer properly documented records of what he has done on a particular job and what he has spent on it. The contractor who maintains accurate and separate business records shows not only that he is serious but also that he can be very convincing in a court or arbitration proceeding. The best way to avoid trials and hearings is to be prepared for them.

## ■ Setting a value for your business

There are times when you need to determine the value of your business: the possible sale of your business, formation of a partnership or other business arrangement with one or more persons, estate and retirement planning, and applying for loans. If you need to determine the value of your business and you have not separated its financial affairs from your personal ones, your job will be very difficult. Businesses are valued in many ways, but their income and expenses are always part of the formula.

> **Legal Reasons for Drawing the Line**
> - Tax laws permit you to deduct all necessary and reasonable business expenses but very few personal expenses.
> - Separation of business expenses will help you comply with your contracts.
> - Keeping track of business expenses separately will allow you to accurately account for all of them.
> - Keeping track of business expenses will assist you in resolving some disputes with customers.
> - If you need to set a value for your business, you'll need to be precise about your business expenses.

## Good-Sense Reasons for Separating Business and Personal Finances

Even if there were no legal or tax requirements for keeping separate records, it's something that you would want to do because it makes good business sense. These good-sense reasons fall into a number of categories that help you:

- Determine what you are really earning

- Decide if your work is worth your while

- Plan for retirement

- Realistically plan for business expansion and major improvements

### ■ So, what am I really making?

The first and most important practical reason to separate business and personal finances is that if you don't do this, you won't be able to tell if your business is really making the money that you expect. When I raise this point with contractors, some of them say, "I can tell if I'm making money if I have 'such and such income' left after taxes at the end of the year." Maybe you can, but why wait until the end of the year?

If you have carefully separated your business and personal finances, you'll easily be able to tell at any time whether your work is making enough money to justify it. But if you haven't, you will surely not be able to do this most of the time and, possibly, you won't be able to do it at the end of the year when you do your taxes.

If you have a spouse who also works out of the home, it becomes even more difficult to decide if your business is making money when finances are combined. I know quite a few contractors who work longer hours than their spouses but find that their take-home pay is much less. This isn't always because their spouses really have a greater take-home pay. Sometimes it's because contractors' business finances are mixed up with their personal finances so they don't really know how much they make.

## ■ Is your work worth your while?

Carrying the previous idea a little further, if you don't keep your records straight, you'll never know if working for yourself is really worth your time. Suppose you are a contractor who finds at the end of

> ### Who's Really Bringing Home the Bacon?
>
> When Harry met Sally, they both knew that running a plumbing business would be a big-time commitment. And it has been, but now they are both wondering if all the time that Harry spends is really paying him as much as they think and whether it's what they want as a family.
>
> In a typical year, Harry and Sally have a combined taxable income of $58,000. Sally earns about $15 per hour in her job as a computer programmer, and she receives medical benefits and small contributions to a retirement plan as well. Harry's medical insurance is on his wife's policy, and he pays the cost of including him and their two children. Harry has no retirement plan of his own and very little savings.
>
> A friend of Harry's with a moderate-size plumbing business has offered Harry a job as a full-time employee at a starting salary of $30,000. If Harry took the job, he would also receive small contributions to a retirement plan. It's very tempting for both Harry and Sally. Although Harry values his independence, this seems like a good opportunity for Harry to make more money and work fewer hours. Harry wants to know if that's true. He can't answer that until he can figure out how much of the $58,000 combined income he brings home. Only by keeping his business records separate can he answer that question.

the year that you're making $20,000 to $25,000 after taxes and all expenses are paid. If you worked between 1,500 and 2,000 hours that year, that translates to an average of $13 to $14 per hour for your hard work. Pretty disappointing, isn't it? You don't need to run a business with all of its headaches and expenses to make that hourly rate. There may be a value to independence, but even independence has limits.

If you could easily earn the same amount of money working for another person or business, with a whole lot less work and aggravation, it's time to seriously think about doing that. Although the tools in this book will help you to make the income that you want, you'll never really know exactly what you are making if you don't keep your business expenses and income separate from your personal life. Take a look at Harry's situation in the sidebar on p. 87.

## ■ Planning for retirement

Another situation where it's important to know the value of a business is when you're considering your retirement plan. Chapter 11 covers the benefits and details that you'll need to know about retirement planning. But you can't begin the process of deciding which plan is best for you unless you have complete and accurate information about the finances of your business. Different forms of retirement plans have different obligations in terms of the money you can or must contribute to them as well as the tax savings that you enjoy. How can you know how much money you really have available for retirement planning if you have combined all of your family incomes and expenses?

## ■ Adding partners or employees

The fourth situation where you need to know everything about the finances of your business is when you're considering adding a partner or employee. When I discuss this matter with contractors, they often say things like, "I know that I have enough work for another guy, but I just don't know if I'll make more money if I hire him." That's a good question to ask yourself before you bring on another person. I've heard of many times when a contractor hires an employee but later realizes that even though he is doing more business, the bottom line is that there is less money left over for him.

Only when you have a clear picture of exactly how much profit you make can you run the numbers to see what the effect would be if you added an employee or brought in a partner. Large businesses make decisions about how many employees to hire by carefully analyzing all financial benefits and costs of each employee. On a somewhat smaller scale, this is exactly what you need to do. Chapter 6 talks about how to do that, but you need to have a clear and accurate picture of your business finances before you can start that process.

> **Planning for Retirement**
>
> John, an excavation and foundation contractor, is married to Helen, who is an assistant buyer for a local department store. Their combined gross taxable income last year was $74,000; Helen's salary at the department store was $39,000. John and Helen use one checking account for everything from monthly mortgage payments and repairs for John's expensive backhoe to groceries and pharmacy items for the house. John billed $86,000 for work last year. He has no tax-qualified retirement plan, but he puts $2,000 to $3,000 into a savings account every year, which he calls the "retirement account." Helen has a very small 401(k) plan through her job.
>
> Every time Helen brings up the subject of retirement, John says, "My expenses are so high that I never see more than half of the money that comes in. How can I put money that I don't have into a retirement plan?" John and Helen's finances are so muddled that it's impossible for John to see how he could be putting money into a tax-qualified retirement plan every year without significantly changing his family's finances.

## ■ Other major improvements

Before you invest in major purchases or improvements, such as replacing your pickup truck or buying expensive tools, you want to be sure that you really have the money available to do that and that the money is coming from your business.

## Methods for Separating Business and Personal Finances

Taxes, legal issues, and sound business choices are the reasons *why* you need to keep your business and personal finances separate. Now, on to the *how*. Once you set up your system, it's pretty simple. There are a few fundamentals:

- Use a business checking account.

- Use a business credit card.

- Don't use your office equipment for personal reasons.

- Don't pay personal expenses from your business account.

## ■ Business checking accounts

A separate checking account for business purposes is absolutely essential. Use this account to pay every single business bill, including bills that may be payable to your family personally. When you buy things for your business and family at the same time, use separate checks whenever possible. The reality, however, is that you can't or won't always do this. That's okay as long as your business pays your family for the business part. Here's how: Pay for the entire item with a personal check and write a separate business check for reimbursement of that portion of the amount that is for the business (including the appropriate part of the sales tax). By doing this, you'll have a complete record of all business expenses in your business checkbook. Be sure that this record includes cash expenditures and their purposes as well.

A properly maintained separate business checkbook ensures that you'll be ready for tax time each year and that you'll also be prepared to prove that you have made payments whenever that may be necessary. Don't be shy about writing a check to reimburse yourself for cash you spent for a business purpose. If you purchase something for your business, you're as much entitled to be reimbursed as anyone else.

Your business checking account must also show deposits of all payments from customers and any other monies such as refunds and insurance payments that come into your business. Some contractors record these payments in their checkbooks as soon as they receive them. There are very easy and inexpensive systems for keeping track of all payments and receipts of small businesses. Some of these are called one-write systems. They help you to record your receipts and payments easily and give you complete information to take to your accountant. And if you have a

---

**Always Pay Yourself Back**

Brendan went to the store to buy a week's groceries for his family. While he was there, he remembered that he was almost out of soft drinks in his office. He keeps a supply of soft drinks in the small refrigerator in his office to offer to clients during business meetings, so they are a business expense. It makes sense for Brendan to pick them up while he is there but writing a separate check for a few six-packs of soft drinks isn't feasible, so he pays for the whole bill from his personal checkbook. But Brendan knows better than to let his family pay for them. When he got home from the grocery, he wrote a business check to himself to pay for the soft drinks. This may seem silly, but these costs add up over the course of a year and *do* make a difference in the profitability of your business.

computer, there are some easy-to-use computer programs that can help you run your business. Some of them include checking, accounts payable, and even job costing.

## ■ Credit card accounts

If you're like most people today, you use your credit cards more than your checking account. So, just as you need a separate checking account, you also need a separate business credit card. Use it only for business expenses. Your monthly business credit card statement will give you a perfect record of your credit card expenses for your business. Look over your statement each month and mark the purpose of each expenditure somewhere on the statement. You could use "gas for pickup" or "paper for fax machine" for items that have to do with general overhead. For expenses related to particular jobs, the name of the customer is typically enough. If you have several jobs for the same customer or several customers by the same name, make a note such as "Jones warehouse job."

If you have any question about what the expense is for, look at the copy of the receipt that you put in your file folder when you bought the item. (Remember, in chapter 4 you learned to write on each receipt what it was for as soon as you made the purchase and to file it in the correct folder.) When you have a separate business credit card and a separate business checkbook, it isn't difficult to keep perfect records.

> **Q:** **What should I do if I accidentally make a purchase that includes some business items and some personal items using my personal checking account?**
>
> **A:** Decide which items are for your business and add up the cost, including sales tax. Make a copy of the receipt for your files. Write a check to yourself for the cost of the business items, and make a note in your checkbook as to what the check was for. File the receipt in the correct folder for your records.

*When you have a separate business credit card and a separate business checkbook, it isn't difficult to keep perfect records.*

## ■ Hands off the office equipment!

Following the suggestions in chapter 3, you should invest in a separate line for your phone/fax. Once you do, be sure to make all of your business calls on that line. And just as important, don't let your family make personal calls from that line, even though it's tempting to do otherwise. When one family member is on your home line, it's easy to duck into your office to make a call from your business line. The same is true for using your fax or copier. Keep your phone, fax, copy machine, and any other equipment and supplies that you have for your business only for your business.

Your business phone and other equipment are costs of doing business. If you share a phone line, you'll need to spend a great deal of time looking over the phone bill each month to separate your business charges from the family charges. With the other office equipment and supplies, you may not be able to separate them at all. Either way, it's a lot of time that you can avoid spending by just keeping them separate in the first place. And don't dismiss the benefits of keeping those business expenses—they can add up to a sizable deduction at tax time.

### ■ Use business accounts only for business

I've stressed the importance of not using your personal account to pay for business expenses. The opposite is just as true. Don't fall into the temptation of paying for personal items through your business account. You'll hear people use the expression "running it through the business," which means paying for something out of your business account that has nothing to do with your business. *Don't do it!* First, charging things to businesses that aren't truly business expenses is a violation of tax laws. Small though it may seem, people have been subjected to all sorts of legal actions because of this. The IRS does not look kindly on tax fraud. Second, you are defeating your goal of running a profitable business. If you "bury" personal expenses in your business account, your business will appear to be less profitable.

Keeping business and personal expenses separate isn't a hard tool to learn to use, but it does take discipline and practice. You'll find that if you stop for a moment each time you spend money to decide whether it's a business or personal expense and if you have both checkbooks and credit cards handy at all times, the process of paying for each expense correctly becomes automatic.

Carefully separating business and personal finances, just as maintaining proper records, may not be the sort of work that is fun for most contractors. If you have help with the office work, you can have your assistant handle this part for you. But however you do this, it is essential if you are to see the greatest possible profit from your business. And you'll find yourself fully prepared for big decisions when you're confronted with them.

**TIP**

**WARNING!**

Don't pay for anything out of your business account that is not really a business expense. This is a violation of tax laws and a very bad business practice.

# CHAPTER 6

# Sizing Up Your Options:
## Corporations, Partnerships, Employees

If your business is growing or if you're establishing a business that is larger than a one-man operation, you're probably considering such questions as:

- Should I incorporate?

- Do I need to hire workers?

- Would a partner help my business?

- Who can help me answer these questions?

These issues have a big impact on the running and profitability of your business. They will probably require that you work with a lawyer and an accountant. More important, they not only affect the way your company operates today but also have an impact on the way it will operate in the future.

Here's what I'll cover in this chapter:

- Future implications: How the decisions you make when setting up your business will be important to future financial stability

- Types of business organizations you can use

- Benefits, drawbacks, and legal issues of forming a corporation or partnership

- What you'll need to do when you use a corporation

- Guidelines to help you make good choices about bringing on employees

- Guidelines for choosing a lawyer

## Look to the Future First

Major business decisions such as what form of business to use, when and if to hire employees, and whether to take on a partner affect your business and personal life for many years to come. Before making major changes, consider where you're headed, both in terms of your business and in terms of your personal life. If you're in your 20s or 30s, it may seem a little unrealistic to consider your plans up to retirement. But if you are older than this or if medical issues have already started to affect your life, you should be evaluating possible future changes all the way through retirement. If spouses, children, parents, or others enter the picture, this becomes even more complicated.

Because there are so many factors in the future over which each of us has no control, making decisions that will affect us for many years is a difficult process. One good way to do this is to look at your business as it is today and then ask yourself some "what if" questions. The "what if" question method is helpful in analyzing the impact major business decisions may have upon future possibilities that you can't predict. You may ask, for example, "If I decide to sell my business in 10 years, will I be better off with or without employees?" or "If my bad back reaches the point where I can't work full time, will I be better off with or without a partner?" See

### Partnering for the Future

Steve, a successful carpenter, is thinking about forming a partnership with his friend, Larry, who is also a carpenter. Steve and Larry have worked on quite a few jobs together and enjoyed the experience. Their discussions about the possibility of a partnership are encouraging, since they seem to have the same objectives and ideas about how to run a business. This sort of a partnership can be beneficial to Steve and Larry in terms of future planning, possible expansion, and increased flexibility in running their businesses. Steve and Larry know that in carefully considering a partnership, they must deal with their future needs in regard to possible disability and retirement.

Individually, each of their businesses is valuable. But if they combine, they gain strength and flexibility in numbers. If Larry were working alone and needed to take an early disability or retirement, the value of his business would be gone because he is the only one contributing to it. However, when partnered with Steve and possibly hiring a few employees, the value of the business continues even if Larry isn't actively involved in the day-to-day work. If Larry became disabled, they could retool their partnership and have Larry do the sales and office work while Steve supervised the job site. It's a win-win situation.

how Steve considered the future benefits of a partner in the sidebar on the facing page.

Exploring each major business decision in this way provides you with an understanding of the pros and cons in terms of your future and not simply present needs. Since the matter of retirement will arise for nearly every contractor one way or another, it's important to consider these questions in light of your retirement plans (see chapter 11 for a discussion on retirement). As a general rule, forming a corporation is a good decision from the standpoint of future planning.

*As a general rule, forming a corporation is a good decision from the standpoint of future planning.*

## Should I Incorporate?

Each state offers a number of legal business forms (corporations, partnerships, sole proprietorships) that a contractor can use. This is an issue that you should discuss with your accountant as well as with a lawyer. I'll cover the various forms available—in a general sense only, since laws vary from state to state—and leave it to you and your lawyer to decide which works best for you. Rather than naming each type, I will refer to the business forms you might use as a "corporation" because that is the most common form used when contractors choose to use a formal business.

Once you have decided which form of business is best for you, in most states you'll need a lawyer to prepare the "Articles of Incorporation," sometimes known as the charter, for filing with your state corporate office along with a few other required documents. This is a relatively simple matter once you have decided upon the best form. The cost varies considerably from state to state and differs depending upon the business form that you choose (such as LLC or corporation). To give you an idea, the filing fees range from $30 to $300, with average legal fees from $500 to $1,000.

### Employer Identification Numbers

Regardless of the type of business form you use, you will need to identify yourself on all your reporting and filing correspondence. You may also be required by your customers to include it on your invoices. If you are a sole proprietor, you can use your Social Security number, but if you have a formal business form, such as an LLC, "S" corporation, or "C" corporation, you will need an Employer Identification Number (EIN), which you can get from the IRS by completing an application (form SS-4). A sole proprietor also has the option of applying for and using an EIN, which would provide more privacy than using a Social Security number. In some states, you have to file an application to get a state identification number as well.

## ■ Types of business forms

There are five main types of business organizations:

■ **SOLE PROPRIETORSHIP:** This is the simplest form of business. One person owns and operates the business. There is no separate legal entity. The owner simply separates the assets of the business from his personal assets. The owner pays all taxes of the business on his personal tax returns. While a sole proprietorship is the simplest form of business, the owner has unlimited personal liability for the debts of the business.

■ **PARTNERSHIP:** A partnership is a separate legal entity, and each partner contributes to the partnership and shares in the profits and losses. The contributions may be in the form of money, skills, property, or other value. Like the sole proprietor, each partner is responsible for his share of the company's taxes and has unlimited personal liability for business debts.

■ **LIMITED LIABILITY COMPANY:** A limited liability company gives you the best of both worlds. It combines a partnership's tax advantage while giving the partners protection from business debts. This form may not be available in your state. Check with your lawyer.

■ **CORPORATION:** There are generally two types of corporations: "C" and "S" corporations: Both are separate legal entities and have shareholders who enjoy protections from personal responsibility. A "C" corporation pays federal and state income taxes on its earnings. When these earnings are passed on to the shareholders as dividends, they are taxed again. This double taxation is one of the drawbacks of a "C" corporation. An "S" corporation generally does not pay income taxes and thus avoids the double taxation.

> **Q:** **What are the benefits of a corporation?**
>
> **A:** ■ Limitations on personal liability
> ■ Tax deductions
> ■ Organizational convenience
> ■ Ease of transfer

## ■ The pros of forming a corporation

There are a number of good reasons for forming a corporation, including liability protection, tax benefits, organizational simplicity, and ease of transfer.

**Liability protection of a corporation**   The greatest benefit of a corporation is the personal liability protection that it provides you. If you are not incorporated and someone brings a lawsuit against your business, your personal assets will be used to pay the settlement costs. But if you use a validly formed corporation and someone brings a lawsuit against it for breaching a contract or causing some form of negligent damage, you (the owner of the corporation) are generally not responsible for what the corporation did.

This is not an absolute rule and certainly should not encourage owners of corporations to be careless about what they are doing. But the protections from liability afforded by corporations are very real and very important in many situations. In the sidebar below, see how this liability protection helped Henry, a roofer. While no contractor wants to lose everything in his corporation, which would include such assets as his pickup truck, his tools, and money in the corporate bank account, risking those things is much better than risking your life savings, your house, and all of your other assets.

Another situation where liability protections of a corporation may be useful is where employees or temporary employees are involved.

---

### Keeping the Roof over Your Head

Henry, a roofer, has the opportunity to bid on a job to put a new roof on a library that contains some very valuable books. The contract specifically states that the library will not be emptied while he is putting on the new roof. Henry had discussed this with the library director and has pointed out the potential hazards to him. If there is a severe storm while he's working under temporary cover, it's possible that some of the books could be damaged. Henry explains that he has both standard and excess liability coverage, but if there were a total loss, his insurance might not cover all of the damage. The library director is willing to take the risk…but Henry doesn't have to.

If Henry were not incorporated, he would be responsible for any damage that isn't covered by insurance. But Henry can enter the contract in the name of a corporation and make it clear in the contract that the corporation alone is responsible for all liabilities that may occur on the job. By doing this, Henry will be able to protect his personal assets from the possibility of liability.

*Even though the times when you need a corporation may be only occasional, once you create your corporation, you will use it for all of your business activities.*

Suppose you normally work alone. You take jobs that you know you can handle, and you know the potential hazards. But if you take on a bigger job and need to hire temporary people, there may be things that are out of your control. What if the person you hire doesn't do the quality of work that you do? What if he makes mistakes or is careless? You may be faced with liability because of defective work or injuries. These are times when having a corporation is a real benefit. Even though the times when you need a corporation may be only occasional, once you create your corporation, you will use it for all of your business activities.

**Tax benefits of a corporation**   Possible tax benefits from incorporating involve deductions that are available for corporations but not for individuals. These deductions include the cost of medical and perhaps other insurance plans and the availability of different forms of pension and profit-sharing plans that permit setting aside income without paying taxes. If you have a corporation and are considering any of these benefits, be sure to discuss the tax implications with your accountant.

**■ TIP**

**USING YOUR CORPORATE NAME**
Be sure that you include your correct corporate name on *all*:
- Contracts and agreements
- Correspondence
- Checks and deposit slips
- Business cards
- Accounts with vendors and suppliers

**Clear, separate identity of a corporation**   Having a corporation helps to make it easier to keep your business and your personal life separate. When you have that "Inc." or "LLC" as a part of your company name, it's hard to confuse your personal and business expenses. Chapter 5 covered the reasons why this is so important from a record-keeping standpoint. This is equally important from a legal standpoint. If you use a corporation to do business, every contract you enter should be in the corporate name. Contractors are often not careful about this, which is a mistake. The difference between "Samuel H. Elkridge" and "Samuel H. Elkridge, Inc." may be the difference between an enormous personal liability and none whatsoever.

Be consistent about using your corporate name in every business transaction. If you are sued, even though you use a corporation, consistently using your corporate name will help you to establish that it's the corporation, and not you personally, that must face the potential liability.

**Ease of transfer of a corporation**   When your business is set up as a corporation, a transfer is very easy. Transfers of corporations are simpler than transfers of interests that individuals hold in their own names. If all of your business assets, property, contracts, and creditors are with your corporation and not with you personally, the transfer of some or all of your ownership of your business is simply a matter of transferring stock. Transferring stock correctly for legal and accounting purposes is almost a no-brainer and requires very little paperwork. There are two basic situations when this would be important:

- Voluntary transfers, such as taking on a partner or selling your business

- Estate planning and involuntary transfers, when an owner dies or the business goes bankrupt

I'll cover taking on a partner shortly and go into estate planning in chapter 11. What's important is that transferring assets, whether in the case of a partnership, passing on an estate, or bankruptcy, is much easier if the assets are held in a corporation.

## ■ The cons of forming a corporation

It may seem to you that forming a corporation is the only way to go. While there are certainly some significant benefits, there are also some drawbacks. As with any other choice you make in your business, the benefits of that choice must exceed the cost of making it. Here are some of the drawbacks:

- **LEGAL ADVICE NECESSARY:**   Forming a corporation means that you'll need a certain amount of legal help at the outset and possibly from time to time. As mentioned previously, your filing and legal fees will probably run $500 to $1,000.

- **ADDITIONAL TAX AND OTHER FILING REQUIREMENTS:**   You will need to file additional tax returns and personal property returns in some states for the corporation every year. While these are not difficult to do, you don't want to add work for no reason.

■ The effect of your choice

The business form comparison chart below gives you an overview of what your choice of business form will mean in the running of your business. Your accountant and your lawyer should address your specific circumstances and the laws in your state. Here are some general rules:

## Comparison of Different Business Forms*

| Feature | Sole proprietor | Partnership | LLC | "C" corporation | "S" corporation |
|---|---|---|---|---|---|
| Separate legal entity | No | Usually | Yes | Yes | Yes |
| Tax return filed | Schedule "C"1040 | Form 1065 | Form 1065 | Form 1120 | Form 1120S |
| Double taxation of dividends | No | No | No | Yes | No |
| Exclude part of dividend income from tax | No | No | No | Yes | No |
| Ease of transfer | Difficult | Difficult | Difficult | Easy | Easy |
| Income taxed at owner level | Yes | Yes | Yes | No | Yes |
| Must use calendar year (generally) | Yes | Yes | Yes | No | No |
| Owners take income out as salary | No | No | No | Yes | Yes |
| Loss deductible from owners' other income | Yes | Yes | Yes | No | Yes |
| Can deduct owners' health insurance | No | No | No | Yes | Yes |
| Owners pay self-employment tax | Yes | Yes | Yes | No | No |
| Must register with Secretary of State | No | No | Yes | Yes | Yes |

*These are general guidelines only. Check with state and federal authorities for current guidelines. Federal requirements are the same throughout the United States, but some states have unique, and sometimes very unusual, provisions regarding the rights and responsibilities of different forms of business. Check with your accountant as discussed in chapter 7.*

- If you decide to use an "S" corporation rather than a "C" corporation, the profits or losses will be passed through to you and any other owners for tax purposes. In this event, the corporation must file a tax return, but it doesn't pay taxes itself. Your accountant will be able to make the correct decision with you at your annual meeting and should also be able to file the necessary "election" form with the IRS within the strict time requirements for doing so.

- Depending upon the type of corporation you use, you'll either receive a W-2 form at the end of each year, showing your wages and tax withholdings in the same manner as a corporation owned by others, or a K-1 distribution form in the same manner as you would receive if you were sharing the profits or losses of a partnership.

For most contractors, the four benefits of incorporating—limitations on liability, tax deductions, organizational convenience,

---

**Checklist: Forming a Corporation**

1. Review the pros and cons explained in this chapter and consider how each of them applies to your business.
2. Use a good accountant who can help you decide which form of business is correct for you.
3. Use a good lawyer to establish the corporation quickly and at reasonable cost.
4. Follow all tax, filing, and reporting requirements.
5. Review all of your business relationships, including customers, creditors, suppliers, banks, insurance companies, and even the Department of Motor Vehicles in your state and the phone company. Notify all of those contacts that you are now using your corporation's name instead of your individual one.
6. Be certain that all future correspondence and financial dealings take place in the corporate name and through your corporate bank account and credit card.
7. Send an inexpensive announcement of your new corporation to all of your customers and others with whom you deal regularly.
8. Don't mix your corporation's business activities with your personal affairs.

and ease of transfer—generally far outweigh the downsides of forming a corporation. As with other planning issues, it's best to make the decision concerning using a corporation before your tax year begins. That way the decision will then be in place, one way or another, for all of your business purposes for the forthcoming year. My experience has been that once a decision to form a corporation is made, virtually no contractors go back to doing business in their own names.

## ▰Business Expansion: Employees, Job Sharing, Subcontractors

Many contractors jump to the conclusion that if they have more work than they can do, they should hire an employee to help them with the overload. But this isn't necessarily true. Very often a contractor who enlarges his business has the same result as the small restaurant owner who doubles the space and tables in his restaurant because it is turning away customers on Friday and Saturday nights. The question is not "Do I ever turn away business?" but rather "Am I always turning away business?" Having a few times when you have more work than you can handle is not sufficient reason to add someone to your payroll.

### ■ Can your work support an employee?

If you take on a full-time employee, there will be times when you can accept jobs that you wouldn't otherwise be able to handle. But you'll also be paying the employee's salary, vacation and sick leave, matching Social Security and Medicare, workers' compensation insurance, unemployment insurance, additional liability insurance, and other expenses *all of the time.*

In addition, there may be other major expenses involved in adding employees, such as new tools or even another truck. Don't forget, too, the amount of time that you will spend training your employee, introducing him to your customers, and coordinating your work schedules. Your time is valuable. If you need to spend it training, you aren't billing it out to a customer, and that's a real cost. When you add up all of these expenses, it's easy to see how the cost of additional employees can quickly outweigh the increased income.

**Q:** If I have more work than I can do, shouldn't I hire someone?

**A:** Not necessarily. You may lose money on an employee even if you sometimes have more work than you can do yourself. Can you keep the employee busy most of the time or just now and then?

Don't hire an employee without doing your homework. You must be convinced that your business has sufficient work on an ongoing basis to justify the cost of that employee. Take a minute and write down your expected income increases along with your expected additional expenses. Look at the new employee income and expense worksheet below, then spend an hour or two with your accountant to review your choices from a strictly financial point of view.

There is no firm rule about how much business you need to justify an additional employee. The value of new business that you can accomplish by having a new employee must be greater than the total of both the direct costs and the increases in general overhead expenses that are associated with that employee.

Don't be surprised if the new employee that you are paying a salary of $35,000 really costs you as much as $60,000 per year when you add all of the benefits, increased overhead, and training time. The question then becomes whether, with the new employee, you will be able to do additional jobs that generate enough money in excess of $60,000 per year to make the whole effort worthwhile. Don't hire a new employee unless you expect to make at least $10,000 more per year than what it costs to keep that employee. The risks and difficulties of a new employee are too great to justify less money for you than that amount.

*Don't hire a new employee unless you expect to make at least $10,000 more per year than what it costs to keep that employee.*

---

**New Employee Income and Expense Worksheet**

Amount of new work
I can do with additional
employee(s)

Expenses for adding
employee(s)

$ _____
$ _____
$ _____
$ _____
$ _____

$ _____
$ _____
$ _____
$ _____
$ _____

Total Gross Income $ _____     Total Expense $ _____

Your total increased income should be $10,000–$15,000 more than your expenses.

Once you are convinced that you have enough work to support an employee, think about how this will change the way you do business. When you hire an employee, you're looking for a relationship that will last a long time. While an employee can make a positive contribution to your business, you will need to take the time to find the right person and then train him. This will take time—time away from your other work. You don't want to invest that time only to have your new person turn around and leave.

While the right employee may be with your business for a long time, the wrong employee or an employee at the wrong time will make your work life very unpleasant, injure your profitability, and, sooner or later, force you to spend time and money deciding the best way to end the relationship. From my perspective, hiring an employee, whether full time or part time, is your last choice in business expansion. Job sharing and using subcontractors are much better choices.

## ■ Job sharing and subcontractors

As your business grows and you find that there are times when you have more work than you can handle, there are a couple of good options for handling the overflow:

- **USING SUBCONTRACTORS:** You can contract out specific portions of a job to another contractor. Usually the contractor does a different type of work than you do, such as carpentry vs. electrical.

- **SHARING JOBS:** You can work together with another contractor (usually doing the same type of work).

The owner with whom you have the contract must agree that this arrangement is acceptable. You can handle this in two different ways. In the sidebar on the facing page, see how Gregg and Susan, both home-improvement contractors, handle their big jobs differently. One shares work with another contractor, and the other uses subcontractors on a selected basis for particular jobs. Both methods enable them to take jobs that would not be possible for a single individual.

A word of caution when job sharing or using subcontractors: The legal line between employees and independent contractors is not

## Two Solutions When You Need Extra Help

Gregg specializes in home improvements and additions. He has a wide range of skills, including carpentry, drywall, laminating, and painting. On many jobs, he'll do everything that's required. On large jobs, however, or on jobs that need to be completed in a relatively short amount of time, Gregg combines his efforts with those of another self-employed contractor whose skills are very much like his own.

Gregg's customers, most of whom are regulars, understand that he'll be doing this and have no difficulty with it. The contract is between Gregg and the owner, and he assumes responsibility for dividing payments between him and the other contractor in a manner that is agreeable to them both. By doing this, Gregg can double the manpower available for particular jobs without any change in his general overhead costs and without hiring an employee.

Susan, on the other hand, deals with the situation of larger jobs by using subcontractors for particular parts of the job. She may, for example, put up the studs for new walls but leave the drywall work to a drywall contractor she engages just for that specific job. She needs, of course, to break out the costs and payments for that portion of the job and see that the subcontractor gets the appropriate payment.

---

crystal clear. Each state has a list of requirements that it uses in determining whether a person is really a subcontractor or an employee. So does the federal government. If your working arrangement fits into the state or federal definition of "employee," regardless of what you and the contractor intended, you may be responsible for federal and state taxes, insurance, and employee withholding. Check with your lawyer on this one.

**Q:** How can you tell if someone is an employee or a contractor?

**A:** There are two key flags in deciding if a person is an employee or a contractor:

- Who decides how the work is done? If you decide how the work is done, not just what work needs to be done, then you might be considered an employer.
- How often do you use this person? If you are using the same person frequently, particularly if you are practically his sole source of income, you could be considered his employer.

# Taking on a Partner

Another way to enlarge your business and achieve the possibility of sharing work is to bring someone in as a partner. Bringing on a partner not only changes the way you do business but also requires a change in your business identity. With a partner, all of the business decisions are joint ones, and you must now think of profits as something to be divided between you and your partner. Even if you continue to own the majority of your business, the issue of how a partner will be compensated in terms of profits will arise sooner or later. If you have been running your business independently, this is a big change—but a change that can have very real short-term and long-term benefits.

## ■ Before you form a partnership

If you are considering a partnership, there are two things you need to do first: work with ("test-drive") your future partner, and review all business details with him.

**"Test-drive" the partner**   It's important to make sure that the person you're thinking of being in business with is someone you can work with day in and day out—on the job and in the office. Make sure that this is someone who has the same work ethic and the same attention to quality as you. Check out the little things, too, including things that don't seem to be directly related to work style. I have seen relationships between partners fall apart because one of them is careful about writing things down and doing things on time and the other is not, or even because one of them smokes and the other does not.

In my experience, the most encouraging thing a contractor can tell me when he's thinking of going into business with another contractor is something like, "Sam and I have been doing quite a few jobs together for the past year or two, and we have been able to talk a lot about our businesses and had a few dinners together with our wives." This sort of remark tells me that the potential partners have kicked the tires, so to speak. They have given themselves the best possible feel for what it would be like to be in business together.

**Review the business details**  Both you and your prospective partner should go over the details of your businesses to see that they are compatible. For example, one of you may have very strong feelings about the need for an expensive medical plan, while the other may want to use the least-expensive HMO in town. One contractor may always use a written contract for his work, and the other may be willing to get into lots of jobs with no written agreement whatsoever. Since your business will only have one medical plan and one policy in regard to written contracts, these are matters that will need to be ironed out if the partnership is to work.

You can use the chapter headings of this book as a general checklist of things to discuss when you are considering a partnership. Matters such as insurance, taxes, retirement programs, and billing and collecting are going to tell you a lot about whether you can run a business with the other person. Bear in mind that there will always be differences in two contractors' handling of these various matters. The important issue is whether in your discussions the differences can be resolved in a way that each of you feels is acceptable for a long period of time.

Be particularly careful about discussing matters involving spending money. A contractor who tries to save every possible nickel on tools, truck repairs, insurance, and everything else does not make a good business partner for a contractor who believes in making reasonable, well-considered expenditures for such things.

## ■ Financial arrangements

The next step is for you and your new partner to consider how to own the business together. Talk with your accountant and go over all of the business details that you have discussed. You will probably need some limited legal advice, particularly to prepare partnership papers.

What you want to consider first is how the business will be controlled and how compensation to you and your partner will be determined. There is no correct formula for either of these things, but it is essential that partners agree upon them. A partnership where either partner feels he doesn't have the control he needs over the business or doesn't earn the proportion of profits he feels entitled to will not work.

There are many options here. Partnerships don't necessarily mean that there will be a 50/50 split of profits. In fact, especially where a corporation is used, there doesn't have to be any relationship between ownership and income. There are owners of corporations who receive no income whatsoever from them and employees of those corporations who have no ownership interest who receive substantial salaries and bonuses. Using a corporation helps in this situation because a corporation may deduct all compensation to its employees that is "necessary and reasonable" for it to do business.

Various tax adjustments that are necessary when individuals own businesses together in their own names or use general partnerships are not necessary in the case of corporations. Where corporations are used, the only monies that are distributed in proportion to ownership are dividends, which are very rarely paid in contracting businesses.

### ■ Future arrangements

To the extent possible, build into your agreement with your partner understandings that take into account possible future changes. For example, your work week may now be 60 hours long while your partner's is 50. This will obviously affect immediate compensation decisions, but it is not unchangeable. A number of things could arise to reduce your work time to less than that of your partner. At that point, compensation for each of you will need to be reconsidered.

An important document between contractors who own a business together, whether it is a partnership, corporation, LLC, or anything else, is a buy-sell agreement. A buy-sell agreement provides for possibilities that are not within the control of one or both owners. These possibilities include death of one of the partners, disability, incompetence, loss of interest in the business, a desire of one partner to sell out, and sometimes other things. It's impossible to know which of these things will occur in the future, but it is possible to agree on what will happen if they do occur.

By asking "what if" questions about each of these situations and discussing the possible answers to those questions, you and your partner can agree upon the framework of a buy-sell agreement. It is then an easy matter to use a lawyer to prepare the buy-sell agreement. The cost, including a meeting and preparation of the buy-sell agreement, should not exceed $750.

### Buy-Sell: How Does It Work?

A buy-sell agreement is a way to handle an unforeseen situation before it disrupts a business. Disability is a good example of how a buy-sell agreement works. Generally when you form your partnership, both partners are working and contributing to the business. They don't expect that one of them will become disabled, but it does happen. Having a buy-sell agreement in place makes it easier for the business to continue.

Since almost all partners agree that they don't want their partners to be replaced by someone else without any choice on their part, buy-sell agreements generally provide for a sale to the remaining partner in the event of permanent disability. The sale will take place at a price that is established by the buy-sell agreement, either in an actual amount, which you agree upon from time to time, or in accordance with a formula that is easy to apply and is typically based upon the value of the business. The buy-sell agreement will obviously have no effect on when a partner becomes disabled, but it will provide an agreed upon means to handle that situation if it occurs.

A written agreement dealing with circumstances where one partner must get out of the business while the other remains will prove essential sooner or later. Get it done at the beginning before difficult times occur.

## Hiring a Lawyer

Throughout this book, I mention various times when you will probably need to talk with a lawyer. If you already have one you've worked with in the past and you are happy with your dealings, keep her. Continuing to work with someone who is familiar with you and your business will be more efficient and economical than starting all over again.

If you don't have a lawyer, read on. You should pick a lawyer as carefully as you do a new car. Over the life of your business, the advice of a good lawyer who has experience in the contracting business could save you the cost of a new car many times over. It's easy to feel a little fearful about choosing and working with lawyers, but remember, the lawyer works for you. Although you are not an expert in the law, you are in the driver's seat when choosing a lawyer.

## ▪ What to look for in a lawyer

You should look for three things when choosing a lawyer:

- **EXPERIENCE WITH CONTRACTORS:** Your lawyer must have experience working in the construction trades and contracting. Many of the issues that you will be involved in are standard matters that your lawyer should already be familiar with. You don't want to pay your lawyer to learn the business.

- **FLEXIBILITY:** Your lawyer must be willing to work on a limited basis. She should be willing to be flexible in working with you and agree to be called upon only when absolutely needed.

- **SIMPLICITY:** Look for a no-frills professional. You can get very good, sound legal and accounting advice from someone who doesn't have a fancy downtown office and lots of secretaries. You may need to look around some, but it will be worth the search.

## ▪ How to find a good lawyer

There are four steps to finding a good lawyer:

1. **ASK FOR REFERRALS:** Talk to as many people in your profession as you can, and ask for names of lawyers whom they have used and whom they like. This is a much better source than relying on phone book listings, advertisements, or the referral services that are maintained by bar associations across the country. The lists of lawyers in each category in the referral services are simply those who ask to be listed. Trade associations make no attempt to distinguish between the good lawyers, the fair ones, and the bad ones.

2. **CONDUCT A PHONE INTERVIEW:** Take the highest-rated names on your list and call them. Use the list of interview questions given in the sidebar on the facing page, adding to it if you'd like, and talk with the lawyers. This is a good screen-

---

**Phone Interview Questions**

Make a list of questions for any lawyer you are considering hiring. Be prepared to ask at least the following questions:

1. Has she had experience with contracting? If yes, how much?
2. Does she have references in the industry?
3. How does she charge? Flat hourly rate or a specific fee for each task?
4. Does she require a retainer (a substantial deposit)?
5. What about phone calls? Are there times when she is available, such as between 2:00 P.M. and 3:00 P.M. each day? How does she charge for phone calls? Typically lawyers charge for a minimum length, regardless of how long the call is. For example, if she bills in quarter-hour increments and you have a two-minute call, you will be charged for 15 minutes.
6. Is she willing to take limited engagements? As you will see in the next chapter, I suggest using an accountant for most of your professional direction. Explain that you are a small contractor trying to keep expenses down and that you will probably only be calling on her for very specific issues that are beyond your abilities. If this isn't okay, this isn't the lawyer for you.

---

ing process that should take 10 to 15 minutes each. If the lawyer doesn't have time for you at this point, she probably won't have time for you once she is working for you. If a lawyer is not interested in the limited engagement, this isn't the one for you. If a lawyer does not want to discuss her hourly rate on the telephone so that you can make comparisons before spending time on a visit, forget her.

3. **CONDUCT A PERSONAL INTERVIEW:** Choose two, maybe three of the lawyers you talked to and ask them each for a free initial consultation. Most lawyers are willing to meet with you once at no charge. The purpose of the personal interview is to give you a chance to meet with the lawyer face to face. She must be someone you feel you can talk with and who really listens to your needs. Are you comfortable in her office or do you feel as though she is talking down to you?

Include in your personal interview a few of the issues that you'll be needing assistance in, such as contracts with owners, forming a formal business, dealing with employees or partners, and legal liabilities. Is the lawyer comfortable with these subjects? You'll quickly learn from her responses whether she is a "book parrot" or someone who really understands your concerns.

If you are not satisfied that the lawyer is willing and able to work on your matter capably, economically, and promptly, thank her for her time and continue your search. You are in the driver's seat—you are choosing to hire or fire her.

4. **MAKE YOUR CHOICE:** Once you've made your choice, call the lawyer and tell her that you want to use her in the future. Ask her what information would be helpful at this point so that she can work with you in the most efficient manner. This may be nothing more than your name, address, phone, and fax, but it also could include the size of your business, how much you earn in a typical year, the type of customers you service, and how you do your jobs, deal with suppliers, and run your business. This should be sufficient information to give your lawyer a good picture of who you are. If the lawyer has more questions, that's a good sign. It means that she's trying to gather enough information to serve you successfully.

The decisions covered in this chapter are some of the most basic and longest-lasting decisions a contractor will make in his business. You are just as capable of making these major decisions as you are of determining whether a particular job is correctly priced and how best to do it. While you will most likely consult with professionals such as lawyers and accountants as you work through these decisions, there is nothing about them that you can't understand and consider fully. Don't be shy about getting help when you need it, and don't be shy about insisting that the help you get is precisely what you need and at a fair price.

No one cares about your business as much as you do, and no one should know more about your business than you do.

# CHAPTER 7

# Taxes:
## Plain and Simple

**T**here are no decisions or issues about running your business that you aren't totally capable of understanding. This is even true about paying taxes. The Internal Revenue Service bears the brunt of a lot of tax jokes because no one enjoys handing over a big chunk of his earnings. But taxes are a part of life, and the IRS filing requirements are pretty straightforward, as are most state requirements. In chapter 4, I went into detail about tracking your income and expenses and record keeping. That's really the toughest part. The rest is knowing which form to use and when to use it.

This chapter will give you an overview of tax requirements and taxation issues that affect contractors. Let me say up front, however, that in my opinion a contractor's time is much better spent doing his trade than it is dealing with the complexities of federal and state tax codes. I highly recommend that you find a good accountant (and a payroll service if you have employees) and let them advise you about tax-related issues and prepare your income tax and payroll tax filings.

The last part of this chapter deals with selecting and working with an accountant. Having a good relationship with your accountant is vital to the smooth and profitable running of your business. This doesn't mean that you can bury your head in the sand when it comes to taxes. You need to be able to have an intelligent conversation with your accountant and payroll service, so you need to have a general understanding of what's involved in the tax cycle.

I recognize, too, that despite my recommendation, some contractors will choose to handle their taxes themselves. In that case, I want to make sure that you have enough information so that you are not taking unnecessary risks. Filing your taxes on time, paying your estimated taxes fully and on time, and making payroll deductions for employee income tax, Social Security, and Medicare are all very serious matters. There are few things that will shut down your business faster than failure to comply with IRS requirements. Even if the IRS doesn't put a lock on your door, you may get smacked with some stiff penalties.

Taxes don't need to be a mystery. With the right information and advice, you'll save yourself a lot of time and money.

### An Expensive Oversight

Maurice, a self-employed plumber who uses an "S" corporation for his business, has never paid his taxes on any sort of schedule. Since Maurice has no employees and has always paid the federal and state taxes he owed when he filed his tax returns, he figured there was no problem with what he was doing. Late in 1998, Maurice received a notice from the IRS advising him that he had not filed his quarterly tax returns properly nor paid the taxes he was required to pay. Maurice vaguely remembered getting a packet of forms from the IRS and also from his state tax office, but he didn't think he really needed to do anything with them. Clearly, the IRS took a different view of things.

The IRS assessed Maurice interest and a penalty for 1998, which totaled $2,371. Maurice thought about talking to an accountant about the matter, but he decided he could save money by speaking with a friend who had had the same experience. His friend told him that the IRS would sometimes forgive the penalty but that he had no chance of bargaining away the interest.

Maurice wound up going to a meeting with the IRS by himself, did get the penalty reduced some, but still had to pay all of the interest. Maurice's final bill from the IRS was $1,782. In addition, Maurice lost a full day going downtown to the IRS and waiting his turn to discuss his problem, plus he spent time making countless phone calls before the meeting. The episode with the IRS cost Maurice about $2,500—not including the taxes. A pretty expensive oversight!

# Tax Estimating and Reporting Requirements

The way you pay taxes and withholding (estimated taxes) is based on the form of business you run. Tax payments can be summed up in a nutshell: If you make money, Uncle Sam wants some of it, and he wants you to pay as you go. Deciding how much you make, how much goes to Uncle Sam, how much goes to your state, and when they should get it is determined by the business form that you have chosen. In addition, if you have employees or if you are considered an employee of your corporation, you will also need to consider Social Security and Medicare withholding, workers' compensation, and unemployment insurance. To make this easy, I've broken down paying taxes into two sections: the basic taxes that you may have to pay and the method and timing for paying them.

---

### Avoiding Penalties

There are very stiff penalties for not paying your estimated taxes on time and for paying less than you should. Here are a few examples:

- Failure to file timely: Up to 25% of the tax due
- Failure to deposit timely: Up to 15% of the tax due
- Failure to pay timely: ½% of the tax due per month, up to 50% of the tax due

In addition to these penalties, the IRS also charges interest on the unpaid taxes.

In general, you must pay taxes on at least 90% of your most recent reported income in order to fall within a "safe harbor" that exempts you from interest and penalties. This is a matter that you should check with your accountant at your annual meeting so that you'll be ready to make the correct reports and payments throughout the next year. It's a good idea to plan to pay 100% of the taxes you anticipate you will owe in the next year—tax refunds are always more welcome than tax bills.

---

## Types of taxes

- **FEDERAL INCOME TAX:** This is the federal tax on your earnings.

- **SELF-EMPLOYMENT TAX:** If you are a sole proprietor or a partnership, this is how you contribute to Social Security and Medicare.

- **PAYROLL TAXES:** Every employer must withhold at least two types of taxes from all employees' pay: federal income tax and the employee's portion of Social Security and Medicare taxes. Most states also have income tax that you need to withhold. Remember, if you are an "S" or "C" corporation, even if you don't have any other employees, you are an employee of your

*If you are an "S" or "C" corporation, even if you don't have any other employees, you are an employee of your corporation.*

corporation. In addition, the employer must pay from its own funds the employer's portion of Social Security and Medicare taxes as well as federal unemployment and state unemployment taxes.

- **STATE SALES TAX:** Some states consider contractors' services to be taxable and require you to charge tax on your invoices. Contact your state retail sales tax office to find out what its requirements are. If your state calls for it, most likely you will have to add the tax to each of your invoices and collect it from your customers, then later pass it on to the state. Your state may require that you get a sales tax permit (and state ID number) that tells your customers that you are authorized by the state to collect the taxes.

## ■ Tax payment requirements

Here's how you will pay the taxes, depending upon your business form:

- **ESTIMATED TAX PAYMENTS:** Sole proprietors, "S" corporations, and some partnerships make quarterly estimated tax payments directly to the IRS using form 1040-ES. You can get these forms from the IRS, which will automatically send future forms to you once you have established a record of earnings. The amounts that you are required to pay in estimated taxes are based on your earnings during the past few years. You will be estimating not only your income tax but also your Social Security and Medicare (self-employment tax). The forms are due with payments on April 15, June 15, September 15, and January 15. Write these dates on your calendar. Don't get behind on your payments, or you'll subject yourself to interest and penalties.

- **TAX DEPOSITS:** If you are a corporation and have sufficient profit, the corporation makes regular estimated tax payments using form 1120W through a commercial bank according to a schedule based on its fiscal year. Again, write these dates on your calendar, and don't get behind on your payments. Don't confuse the tax liability of the corporation with your personal

## A Year in the Life of a Taxpayer

Nick owns an electrical contracting business, Nick's Electric, LLC. He's been in business for three years and does all the work himself. For the last few years, his business has made a profit of just about $40,000. Between his and his wife's income, they are in the 28% tax bracket. He used the 1040-ES worksheet. The worksheet walks him through all of the calculations, but essentially, it looks like this:

Taxable income after exemptions
  and deductions:                        $30,050
His estimated income tax per year:  $8,414 (30,050 × 0.28)
His Social Security/
  Medicare contribution             $5,630 [(40,000 × 0.92) × 0.153]
Total estimated taxes               $14,044

Nick marks the dates on his calendar and sends the IRS the estimated tax on the following dates.

Payment 1 (1040-ES) is $3,511—due on April 15
Payment 2 (1040-ES) is $3,511—due on June 15
Payment 3 (1040-ES) is $3,511—due on Sept. 15
Payment 4 (1040-ES) is $3,511—due on Jan. 15

Since Nick is a single-member LLC, he is able to file a joint 1040 with his wife and put his business expenses on a Schedule C. In January he meets with his accountant and brings with him all of his income and expense records for his business, along with his personal records. His accountant prepares his 1040 and Schedule C. Nick has overpaid the IRS by $150, so he will get a refund.

tax liability. If you are an employee of your corporation, your estimated tax payments are handled by payroll taxes.

- **PAYROLL TAXES:**   If you have employees, you must report the collected income, Social Security, and Medicare taxes for each reporting period. There are two forms that you use to pay these on a regular basis. The "Federal 941 deposit" reports federal withholding and Federal Insurance Contributions Act (FICA) taxes, which include Social Security and Medicare. The "Federal 940 deposit" reports Federal Unemployment Tax Act

> **Payroll Services**
>
> Using a payroll service can be a good investment, even if you only have a few employees. A service computes the necessary federal and state withholding required for each employee, as well as FICA and the employer's matching FICA. It stays up to date on all the payroll tax regulations, saving you a tremendous amount of time. You can use a service to make payments of withholding directly to the federal and state taxing authorities with no further action on your part.
>
> Not only does a service process the payroll, make the necessary deductions, cut the checks, and even furnish W-2 statements, but it also gives you a full record of your salary expenses for income taxes. Shop around and don't be afraid to ask questions about the most economical packages.

(FUTA) taxes, which are used for unemployment compensation. Use form 8109 coupons, which the IRS provides, to make your required 940 and 941 payments. The coupon book includes instructions about how to complete and where to make the deposit (generally at a commercial bank). Once a year, you must file form 940 and forms W-2 and W-3, which tell both the government and your employees about their incomes and tax withholdings. If you use a payroll service, it can handle all of this for you.

- **STATE SALES TAXES:** If your state (or the state that you are doing the work in) requires that you collect state sales tax, you will have to add that amount to all of your contracts and invoices and pay the state sales tax to your state taxing authority in accordance with its requirements. Find out about state requirements for collection and reporting. You may have to make special deposits to certain banks to report this tax. When you are looking at your income, remember that the sales tax that you collect and hand over to the state is not taxable income.

- **1099s:** If you have used subcontractors rather than employees, you may be required to report their incomes to the federal government using a 1099 for each. Both the government and the subcontractor get copies.

## ■ State and city requirements

State tax requirements (and sometimes city requirements, too) generally follow the federal tax requirements, but they differ somewhat from state to state. In some states, for example, you must make estimated tax payments on a quarterly basis, just as you do to the federal government. Find out from your accountant or state tax authorities what those requirements are and follow them.

### Fingertip Tax Guide

| TYPE OF BUSINESS | TAX | FORM TO FILE | DUE DATE |
|---|---|---|---|
| Sole proprietorships & single-member LLCs | Federal income tax filing | Schedule C or Schedule E* (form 1040) | Same as 1040 (April 15 for calendar-year individuals) |
| | Self-employment tax filing | Schedule SE (form 1040) | Same as 1040 |
| | Estimated tax payments | 1040-ES | April 15, June 15, September 15, and January 15 (assuming a calendar year) |
| Partnerships and multimember LLCs** | Federal income tax filing | Schedule E (form 1040) | Same as 1040 (April 15 for calendar-year individuals) |
| | Self-employment tax filing | Schedule SE (form 1040) | Same as 1040 |
| | Annual return of income— information filing | Form 1065 | April 15 for calendar-year partnerships and multi-member LLCs |
| "S" corporations | Federal income tax filing | Form 1120S | 15th day of 3rd month after end of tax year |
| "C" corporations | Federal income tax filing | Form 1120 or 1120A | 15th day of 3rd month after end of tax year |
| | Estimated tax payments | 1120W (deposits made with commercial bank or through electronic payment) | 15th day of 4th, 6th, 9th, and 12th months of tax year |

*The schedule depends upon the type of business.
**Individuals pay estimated taxes if they are members of LLCs, partners in partnerships, or owners of "S" corporations.

## Free Forms and Publications from the IRS

- Schedule C, Profit or Loss from Business
- Schedule SE, Self-Employment Tax
- Form SS-4, Application for Employer Identification Number
- Form 1040-ES, Estimated Tax Form for Individuals
- Form 4562, Depreciation and Amortization
- Form 8829, Expenses for Business Use of Your Home
- Publication 463, Travel, Entertainment, Gift, and Car Expenses
- Publication 334, Tax Guide for Small Businesses
- Publication 505, Tax Withholding and Estimated Tax
- Publication 525, Taxable and Non-Taxable Income
- Publication 533, Self-Employment Tax
- Publication 535, Business Expenses
- Publication 583, Starting a Business and Keeping Records
- Publication 946, How to Depreciate Property
- Publication 910, Guide to Free Tax Services

# For the Do-It-Yourselfers

If you want to know more about tax matters, look in the business/taxes section at your local bookstore and you'll probably find a number of shelves holding tax guides. Look for the ones that are written specifically for small businesses.

A good source of free (and accurate) information is the federal government. You can look in the phone book under U.S. Government for your local IRS office, where an agent can answer questions and give you all of the necessary tax forms and the tax publications that explain them. You could also call the IRS toll-free at (800) 829-1040 to order the forms or use the worldwide web at http://www.irs.ustreas.gov.

Some of the most important tax forms are listed above. Also included on the list are some free IRS publications on subjects of particular value to small business owners. The publication on depreciation and home business use, for example, can help you substantially lower your taxes. Since most state taxing laws mirror federal laws except in a few small matters, the information from the IRS can be useful for both purposes. Many states, however, do have their own instruction booklets available, so check with your state taxing offices.

*The most important part of your tax filing is keeping good records and documenting your income and expenses.*

## ■ Want to do your taxes yourself?

Although I don't recommend that you do your own taxes since I think that your time is better spent in your trade, it's certainly possible, especially if you don't have any employees. If you are inclined to do that, you should seriously consider using a good tax preparation computer program. There are a number of them on the market that are easy to use, include many of the needed tax forms, and cost well under $100. Just look in your local computer store or software catalog.

# ▰Tax-Related Issues for Contractors

While it's beyond the scope of this book to go into all of the details of tax preparation, there are a few "hot buttons" that you should look out for as you are keeping your tax records and preparing your information for your accountant. The most important part of your tax filing is keeping good records and documenting your income and expenses.

Chapter 4 covered record-keeping issues and deductible expenses. There you learned to make a folder for each of your income and expense categories. By keeping these records, you ensure that you will get all the deductions to which you are entitled and that you can support these deductions in the event the IRS audits your return. These categories are basically those that are listed on the IRS Schedule C, Profit and Loss from Business, which you may file depending upon the type of business that you use. Following are some of the most important deductions and those that are easily overlooked.

## ▪ Depreciation and Section 179 election

In general, capital expenditures (major investments in your business that are not used up in a short time) need to be depreciated over the expected life of the item. For example, a computer or a truck would be a capital expenditure because these items last a number of years and add value to your business. Fax paper or nails are used up quickly and add no long-term value to your business. The IRS has rules that cover how long

### Standard Deductions for Contractors

Here are some of the standard deductions that apply to contractors:

- Supplies
- Tools
- Advertising
- Depreciation
- Insurance
- Meals and entertainment (as part of your work)
- Dues to professional organizations
- Subscriptions to professional magazines
- Transportation expenses (but not commuting to and from work)
- Special work clothes
- Fees for professional services, such as an accountant and lawyer, and other fees
- Wages, benefits, etc., related to employees
- Home office expenses
  - ❏ Phone/fax/cell phone bills and equipment
  - ❏ Fax/copy machine and supplies
  - ❏ Computer and supplies
  - ❏ Office supplies (paper, pens, pencils, etc.)
  - ❏ Beverages for business guests
  - ❏ Mortgage interest
  - ❏ Utilities (gas, electric, oil, and water)
  - ❏ Real estate taxes
  - ❏ Household insurance

*For the small contractor, the important thing to remember is the Section 179 Property election.*

different types of equipment are expected to last and formulas for depreciating them over their expected life. The IRS or your accountant can help you with these.

For the small contractor, the important thing to remember is the Section 179 Property election. For capital expenditures that qualify, the IRS allows you to take the entire deduction up to a certain amount in the first year of your purchase. Deducting the entire cost of something that is purchased in one year, which is known as *expensing*, is always worth a good deal more money than depreciating the cost of the same item over a number of years. For the year 2000, the amount is $20,000, and that amount increases in subsequent years.

Since many of the larger items you must buy for your business are Section 179 Property, a little planning may make it possible for you to make maximum use of this deduction. You can learn what is considered to be Section 179 Property by calling the IRS or by reading its publications. If you need to buy more than $20,000 worth of such property, you might decide to spread your purchase over two or more years in order to get the full value of this deduction in each of those years.

## ■ What contractors overlook

Certain types of business expenditures are overlooked far more often than others. Very few contractors forget to keep track of their expenditures for tools, big supplies, insurance, and expenses of their trucks. But smaller items, such as the nails that you pick up on your way to the job site, are often overlooked—even though they are things that you use all the time. In addition, many contractors don't take advantage of the home-office deduction, Section 179 Property deductions, and deductions for items that concern relatively informal dealings with other contractors. In the sidebar on the facing page, see how missing small deductions cost Frank, a roofer, big money at tax time. Contractors, like most small business people, often don't keep good track of cash expenditures that qualify for deductions. Listed on p. 124 are some of the deductions that contractors often overlook.

### Like Giving Money to Uncle Sam

At almost every turn in his work, Frank, a roofer, misses an opportunity to take a tax deduction. Here's a typical scenario for him. He has taken a job to put a new roof on a two-story house. Since Frank doesn't do gutters, he will have Kevin do the gutters and downspouts for an agreed part of the contract price. Twice during the job, Frank and Kevin have lunch at Frank's expense to discuss how they will coordinate their work.

During the job, Frank's hydraulic nailer stops working, but luckily, a local repair dealer repairs the nailer for only $37.82. When an unexpected rainstorm arrives during the job, Frank needs to buy an extra tarpaulin from Kevin for $20. Frank lost more than $100 worth of tax deductions just on this job because he didn't bother to get receipts for the tool repair, the tarpaulin, and the business lunches with Kevin.

In addition to the deductions that he misses while on the job, he often picks up supplies for his work when at the grocery store and doesn't bother to break out the business expense from his family's food.

When you add up all of these over the course of a year, Frank loses about $2,000 worth of deductions. In Frank's tax bracket, these deductions would be worth about $400 to him. Since Frank's hourly rate is $40, Frank gives the government a gift of 10 hours of his work time every year.

## Selecting the Right Accountant

Of all the professional business relationships that you will need (lawyers, insurance brokers, financial advisors, accountants), far and away the most important is your accountant. An ongoing relationship with a good accountant will serve a variety of important purposes for you.

### How an accountant can help

There are a variety of issues that your accountant can and should help you with. These include taxes, corporation filings, and retirement plans.

**Taxes** I recommend that you use a certified public accountant who has experience with contractors to handle your tax matters. While it's certainly possible to do your own taxes—especially if you are not incorporated and have no employees—it's not the best use of your time and talent. You are trained and capable in your trade, just as your accountant is in hers. She is much better prepared to see all of the tax implications and benefits and to defend your tax filing, if that becomes necessary.

An accountant is not the least expensive person who can do your tax filings, but the advantages that you will gain from using an accountant are worth the difference. There are tax preparers and enrolled agents (EAs) who can also process tax returns, but my

---

### Don't Overlook These Deductions

- Home-office deduction available to most contractors who have no other office.
- Expenses related to work that is done at home, such as paper and fax supplies, separate phone and fax phone bills, drinks in your office refrigerator, and other miscellaneous items.
- Section 179 Property deductions. Contractors often depreciate items that qualify for this special treatment as expenses. Contractors also often fail to plan for the purchase of Section 179 Property to provide them with maximum deductions.
- Cash purchases, sometimes even including gas for the business truck or generator. Especially when you pay cash, get a receipt and write on it what it was for.
- Items that you buy when shopping for groceries. Since many supermarkets carry some of the items contractors use for their work, it's easy to pick them up and forget to keep track of them.
- Expenses for casual business meals. You don't have to be wearing a suit for the meal to be deductible. If there's a real business purpose to the meal, it's typically deductible.
- Special deductions related to building or improving certain types of structures. These rules are fairly complicated, but materials available from the IRS and, of course, information from your accountant will explain them.
- Items purchased from other contractors in the course of doing jobs. These are easy to overlook.

recommendation is to find a good certified public accountant who will handle not only your taxes but also other financial and business matters.

Your accountant will help you make sure that you accurately track all of your income and expense records and that you get every possible deduction that you're entitled to. She will meet with you once a year to go over everything and make any necessary adjustments.

**Corporation filings**  Your accountant should offer advice on setting up your legal business form (corporation, LLC, sole proprietorship) and be responsible for keeping your federal and state tax filings and corporate filings up to date, especially if you use a corporation. Your accountant will help you with matters such as deciding what tax status to claim for a corporation if you use one and how best to handle other people who do work on your jobs.

**Retirement plans**  Finally, your accountant should assist you with maintaining your qualified retirement plan, which will be discussed in chapter 11. Some accountants are sufficiently knowledgeable to help you in establishing a retirement plan and qualifying it with the IRS for appropriate tax treatment.

**Q:** **What should I look for in an accountant?**

**A:** In addition to preparing your tax returns and other required tax filings, your accountant should be able to:

- Help you decide the type of corporation or other formal business that might be useful to you.
- Help you keep all necessary filings of your corporation or other formal business up to date.
- Be available to answer questions that arise from time to time in your work.
- Understand the special needs of contractors.
- Help you in an economical fashion.
- Assist you in selecting the appropriate qualified retirement plan for your purposes and qualifying that plan with the IRS.
- Help you with filings and issues involving your retirement plan.

## ■ How to choose an accountant

Select your accountant using the same techniques that you use when finding a lawyer (see pp. 109–112). Get recommendations from business associates and friends, then interview your prospects both over the phone and in person. When you select an accountant, ask questions about her experience and willingness to work with taxes, corporate issues, and retirement planning. You want an accountant who is familiar with the work of contractors and understands your special needs. You also want an accountant who is conscious of the

*When you select an accountant, ask questions about her experience and willingness to work with taxes, corporate issues, and retirement planning.*

cost of her services to you and can help you avoid unnecessary expenses whenever possible.

Since nearly all accountants charge for their work on an hourly basis, the objective is to use your accountant as little as possible but a sufficient amount to enable her to help you with all the necessary matters. A good accountant will assist you with record-keeping matters only to the point where you're able to handle these entirely by yourself.

## ■ Using your accountant effectively

It's important that you have at least one annual meeting with your accountant. If you're going to have only one meeting, it should be as close to the end of the year as possible. You will want to check with your accountant once or twice during the year to see that your tax payments are sufficient in light of your income, but this does not require a meeting. The annual meeting should cover each of the subjects with which your accountant is assisting you and enable you to plan properly for the forthcoming year.

**Preparing for discussions with your accountant**   In addition to careful selection of your accountant, you'll receive the best and least expensive service from her if you prepare properly for discussions with her. Most of your discussions will be by phone, and hopefully they will be brief. When you call your accountant to ask a question, have all the documents you need available. Be certain to fax copies of those documents with a brief cover explanation to her before the phone call.

For example, if you need to complete a business form and don't understand some of its questions, fax the form to your accountant with a memo like this: "Martha, I need to ask you a few questions about how to complete this form. I'll give you a call this afternoon, probably after 3:00 P.M. Thanks. Fred." This gives your accountant all of the information she needs to answer your question before you even call. It'll save you time, save your accountant time, and, best of all, save you money. In the sidebar on the facing page, look at how Jerry the carpenter saved a lot of money with a quick fax to his accountant. It doesn't take many incidents like this to save enough

### Using Your Accountant to Save Money

Jerry, a carpenter, has an expensive bench saw that he brings to nearly every job site. Jerry uses the saw for everything from ripping long boards to mitering fine pieces of trim. After 12 years of continual use, the saw finally broke. Since a new saw would be a big investment—more than $5,000—Jerry wanted to be sure that he bought the saw in the best way for his tax situation. But he certainly didn't want to spend a lot of money for the time of his accountant, Martha. Jerry faxed the dealer's information to Martha with a cover sheet that said:

"Martha: My great bench saw finally gave out. I need to replace it with a new model. Enclosed is the cost. Is there anything special I should do to help my taxes? I'll give you a call at the end of the day. Jerry."

Within two hours, Martha sent the following fax back to Jerry: "Jerry: Don't buy the saw until 2001, if you can wait, since you have used up your tax benefits for this year. Get it any time on or after January 1, 2001. My rough calculation is that this is worth nearly $1,000 to you, bottom line. Happy New Year! Martha."

money for you to pay the accountant's entire bill for the year and get all of the services discussed in this chapter.

Throughout this book, I've talked about good business practices and the business tools that you use to run your business effectively. Paying your taxes on time and in full, whether it's estimated payments, filings, or withholdings, is not just good business practice—it's the only practice or you won't have a business. You need to master these tax tools so that you will understand what your accountant is doing or, if you do it yourself, so that you will do it correctly.

Taking the time to find a good accountant who can work with you on tax and other financial issues is one of the best time investments you'll make in your business. You'll have an ally who will guide you in your business decisions, protect you from unnecessary fines and penalties, and make sure that your business enjoys every deduction it deserves. When April 15 rolls around each year, you can be on your job making money, not sweating over your taxes.

*Taking the time to find a good accountant who can work with you on tax and other financial issues is one of the best time investments you'll make in your business.*

# CHAPTER 8

# Insurance:
## Money Well Spent

Insurance is one of the most expensive business investments you will make. It's frustrating because you spend a lot of money, have what seems like nothing to show for it, and, hopefully, will never use it. This gives most people the feeling that they're paying for nothing. One contractor told me, "I don't really think my job is very risky. I've only had one claim against me in 20 years, and that was for knocking over an antique cabinet trying to get to a wall outlet. It cost me $200."

*Just as you wouldn't consider going without auto insurance for your family car or homeowner's insurance for your home, you can't afford to be without adequate insurance for your business.*

The problem is that as a contractor you take risks all the time that you probably aren't aware of. If you were to injure someone while doing your work or seriously damage expensive property, you could be responsible for the medical expenses of the injured person or for the repair or replacement of the property. These costs, along with the legal fees, would surely be more than you could afford and could bankrupt your business and possibly affect your personal assets.

Just as you wouldn't consider going without auto insurance for your family car or homeowner's insurance for your home, you can't afford to be without adequate insurance for your business. Although you may suffer sticker shock when you first price your liability and workers' compensation coverages, insurance is the only way to manage the economic burden of a large loss so that you or your company won't be financially devastated by it.

This chapter will cover basic types of insurance, which I'll put into two broad categories: insurance to protect your business and insurance to protect your employees. Insurance to protect your business is typically required by your clients and by good business judgment. Insurance to protect your employees is generally required by state laws. I'll go into the forms of liability and other business coverages, workers' compensation, and unemployment insurance. Because of the complexity of the topics, I'll cover medical and disability coverages separately in chapters 9 and 10. Since insurance issues can be every bit as complicated as tax or legal topics, you should find a good insurance broker who can explain the benefits and restrictions of the policies you are considering.

## Types of Insurance

Three types of insurance you should have are general liability and related business coverages, workers' compensation, and unemployment.

- **LIABILITY INSURANCE:**
  This type of insurance protects you in the event that you injure other persons or damage property while doing your work. In addition to your basic liability policy, there are other coverages that you can add to provide more complete protection for your business. Various states require contractors to maintain particular amounts of general liability insurance. In addition, many states have laws requiring contractors to maintain bonds to protect customers from defective work. Bonds, which are purchased from insurance companies, offer what is known as *surety protection*. In general, construction businesses and

---

**Insurance Action Checklist**

1. What kinds of insurance do you need to protect your business?
   - General liability
   - Excess liability (umbrella policy)
   - Builder's risk
   - Business auto
   - Nonowned auto
   - Equipment theft
2. Do you have employees? If so, check on workers' compensation and unemployment insurance.
3. Find a good independent insurance broker who has experience with contractors and discuss the options, choices, and prices that apply to each form of insurance.
4. Make folders in your file box for each form of insurance that you require and be certain to include in each folder a complete copy of each of your insurance policies.
5. Ask your broker to explain how to make claims and give notices so you will be prepared when the time comes. Follow the policy's procedures exactly, and keep copies of all claims correspondence.
6. Decide whether each insurance cost is part of your general overhead or a cost that applies to a particular job. Establish your hourly rate and your pricing for each job accordingly.

often the individuals who own them must guarantee to reimburse the bonding company if it is called upon to pay the claim of a customer.

■ **WORKERS' COMPENSATION:** Workers' compensation provides payment to workers who are injured on the job or who become ill because of their job. The laws of your state strictly govern this coverage.

■ **UNEMPLOYMENT INSURANCE:** Unemployment insurance provides temporary income to people who have lost their jobs. This helps them financially while they are looking for a new job. As with workers' compensation, the laws of your state govern this coverage.

## Insurance to Protect Your Business

The starting point for insurance for contractors is comprehensive general liability (CGL) insurance. In addition, you will need builder's risk, business vehicle, equipment theft, and nonowned auto coverage.

### ■ Comprehensive general liability

There are three basic components to your comprehensive general liability policy: the risks covered, the limits of liability, and the exclusions. A good insurance broker with experience with contractors can help you understand what your policy covers and what it doesn't. Your broker will be your final authority in this, but the following will give you some general explanations.

■ **RISKS:** Generally, your CGL covers a number of risks, whereby your company may be put into financial jeopardy because of an accident or unplanned situation. Two of the more common risks are medical liability and property damage liability. If you were to injure a person while you were working and that person sued your business for the medical and related expenses, your medical liability insurance would pay some or all of those expenses, including your legal and other related fees. If you were to damage some property and the person who owned that property sued your business for the cost of replacement, repair, or other related expenses, your property damage liability insurance would pay some or all of those expenses. A good CGL policy will cover most of the risks that apply to contractors (see the sidebar on p. 132 for a list of the most common policy features in a CGL policy).

- **LIMITS OF LIABILITY:** This is the maximum amount the insurance company will pay per occurrence or in total. Liability insurance policies generally have two limits of liability: the "per occurrence" limit, which is the maximum amount the insurance company is required to pay for any particular incident; and the "aggregate" limit, which is the maximum amount the insurance company is required to pay for all incidents. (Sometimes these two limits are the same.) Limits of liability apply for each policy year. Suppose, for example, you had a $500,000/$1 million CGL policy for a particular year and you had two large negligence claims against you during that year. Your insurance company would not be required to pay more than $500,000, attorneys' fees and costs included, for either of the large negligence claims against you. It also would not be required to pay more than $1 million for both claims together.

For small contractors, general liability policies tend to have limits of $1 million for everything, but discuss your individual situation with your broker. Since your legal costs are included here and they can

*A good CGL policy will cover most of the risks that apply to contractors.*

### Careless Oversight, but Financial Disaster Avoided

Henry, a painting and wallpaper contractor, is hanging wallpaper in a formal, wainscoted dining room. Because of the intricacy of the fabric, it will take Henry two and a half days to do the job. There is a double door that connects the dining room to the living room. For ventilation, Henry leaves the double doors open while he is working. At the end of his first day, he leaves all of his supplies and equipment on his temporary work table in the dining room, but he leaves the double doors leading to the living room open.

As you can imagine, this is an accident waiting to happen…and it doesn't take long. During the evening, the owners' young child wanders into the dining room, grabs one of the mat knives, and cuts his hand. Fortunately, the child is not critically injured, but his hand requires emergency treatment and a fair number of stitches. Henry's oversight, however, could have fatally injured his business. Because of the accident, the owners filed a suit seeking not only to recover the cost of their child's medical care but also money for his pain and suffering and for their own mental distress—a total in excess of $1 million!

Whether Henry winds up being found liable or not, this case could drag on for years, and he will have legal expenses and costs probably running into the tens of thousands of dollars. Fortunately, Henry has a general liability insurance policy that covers this incident. His insurance company will cover his liability and his legal costs.

**A Good CGL Should Have:**

- Coverage for the kinds of situations that are likely to happen in your line of work.
- Clear identification of the "insured persons" covered by the policy. These should include your business, you, and all other employees of the business.
- Sufficiently high limits of liability in light of the risks you are taking. These should be not less than $500,000 per incident and $1 million in the aggregate.
- Reasonable exclusions. If your policy excludes situations that are typical for you, then the policy is virtually useless.
- Geographic coverage that is sufficient in light of where you work. If, for example, you work in more than one state, the coverage provided by the CGL policy must be available in each state where you work.
- No restrictions or conditions that you can't always abide by. For example, if you normally leave your tools at the job, don't accept a policy that does not cover you if you do.

be a big part of your claim, you want to be sure that you're adequately covered in the event of a major claim. If you're doing work that presents possible risks greater than $1 million, look into what is known as an "excess" or "umbrella" liability policy. An excess policy provides coverage over and above your basic limits—it doesn't duplicate your basic limits. If you have a $1 million basic policy and a $5 million excess policy, your basic policy pays the first million and then the excess policy pays the next $5 million for a total coverage of $6 million. It will be up to your broker to make sure that your basic and your excess policies work together properly so that there are no gaps in your coverage.

- **EXCLUSIONS:** These are the risks that are not covered by the policy. Most policies have some exclusions, which generally apply to those types of losses that are relatively rare and rather expensive to pay for, such as flood or nuclear disaster. If all exclusions were covered on your policy, the cost to you would be much higher. Ask your broker to explain the exclusions to you and discuss with her the type of work that you do. It may be that one of the exclusions applies to the kind of work that you do and you should see if it is possible to waive, or remove, the exclusion by paying more for your policy.

- ## Builder's risk

If you build additions to existing structures or new structures, you'll need liability insurance that is designed to cover your projects while they are under construction. This is referred to as "builder's risk" or "course of construction" insurance. Depending upon the type of work that you do, you may have this coverage as part of your policy or you may just add it now and then to cover specific projects. If you are required to have it for a specific project, you can either have your customer provide and pay for the coverage or you can include the cost in the bill to your customer (see "Including Insurance Costs in Your Prices" on pp. 140–141).

## ■ Business vehicle coverage

The other form of insurance for contractors that is always required is insurance for your vehicle. Since your vehicle, probably a pickup truck, is used for work, it is a commercial vehicle and subject to commercial insurance rates. There are different categories depending upon how you use your truck, and the differences in cost can be substantial. Talk this over with your broker to make sure you are placed in the lowest category for which you qualify. There are two types of commercial auto insurance to consider: liability and physical damage.

**Business vehicle liability**  The liability portion is similar to the general liability discussed previously—it covers injury or damage to property that you cause while using your truck. In many states, liability coverage is mandatory but only at very low limits. Ignore those minimum limits. I strongly recommend that all contractors have vehicle insurance of at least $250,000 per occurrence/$500,000 aggregate. Adequate liability coverage is particularly important because people who drive business vehicles are sometimes targets for suits involving a great deal of money because some people

---

### Read the Fine Print—Common Exclusions

Your CGL policy probably won't cover your damages (the amounts that you might have to pay) in the following situations:

- Extraordinary occurrences, such as hurricanes, floods, nuclear disasters, or acts of war.
- Intentional wrongdoing.
- "Gross negligence." Avoid this if you can because "gross negligence" is frequently confused with "negligence," or normal oversights.
- Use or storage of hazardous materials. Be careful on this one. Some of the chemicals found in common equipment such as air conditioners as well as some solvents and glues are considered hazardous.
- Use of certain equipment or the failure to use certain equipment. For example, you might not be covered if you use a certain type of scaffold or if you allow people not wearing safety goggles on the work site.
- Acts of persons who are not specifically listed as a covered person ("named insured") on your policy. You could be sued, for example, for damages caused by one of your independent contractors, who is not a named insured. The way to protect against this is to require all of your independent contractors to include your company, you, and your employees as named insureds on their insurance policies while they are working for you.

**TIP**

**BUSINESS VEHICLE LIABILITY**

If you have an excess liability policy, ask your broker how your commercial vehicle policy works with it—you don't want to pay for coverage that you don't need.

assume that business owners are wealthy. If your driving record is good, you may find that the cost of a higher liability limit is not that great.

**Commercial vehicle physical damage**   There are two types of coverage that insure damage to your vehicle, as opposed to covering your responsibility for injury or damage to someone else (liability). They are collision and comprehensive coverage.

- Collision covers damage to your truck if you are involved in an accident. It is generally used only if you are at fault.

- Comprehensive covers damage to your truck that is not caused by an accident. This includes such things as damage to your windshield from a rock thrown up from the road, acts of nature, and damage while your truck is parked.

---

### Use Deductibles, but Don't Bet the Ranch

Tommy, a wood-flooring contractor, has never had a claim against him in 17 years. He doesn't take jobs unless the area of the house where he is working is thoroughly cleared. His standard contract, signed by every owner who hires him, says that no one will enter the rooms where he is working until the job is complete.

For many years, Tommy's CGL policy cost him only a few hundred dollars a year. Last year, however, partly due to the fact that Tommy hired his first employee and partly due to changes in the insurance market, the policy premium went up to $1,400. To lower the premium, his broker suggested that he raise his deductible from $100 to $1,000. This would reduce his premium by almost $600 per year with no other change in his coverage.

That's what Tommy did. Since he had never had a claim and didn't think it was likely that he would, the savings on his annual premium made it worth taking the additional annual risk. In only two years at present rates, Tommy will save more than the $900 additional risk he was taking for each claim. The most important thing about Tommy's reasoning was that the additional risk he took to save money was a risk that he could afford. You should take reasonable risks when you can afford to take them, but never take a risk that is a "bet-the-ranch" risk.

Most collision and some comprehensive policies involve a deductible, which is the amount that the policy owner agrees to pay out of pocket for each claim. For example, if your policy has a $500 deductible and you had $10,000 worth of damage to your truck, you would pay the first $500 and your insurance company would pay the remaining $9,500. However, with that same policy and $500 deductible, if you had a loss of $350, your insurance would pay nothing. The higher the deductible, the lower the premium (cost of insurance). Choose a deductible that is high enough so that your insurance is affordable but not so high that you couldn't possibly afford to pay it if you needed to.

Insurance is meant to help prevent financial disaster for you and your company. It's not meant to be a maintenance contract. If you use it like that, you are spending more than you need to for your insurance. In the sidebar on the facing page, see how Tommy saved himself a lot of money by carrying a pretty high deductible. If your truck is so old that the book value is lower than the cost of the collision insurance, it's probably not worth carrying collision coverage. It's more economical in this case to pay for the repairs yourself.

> **TIP**
>
> **THEFT FROM UNATTENDED VEHICLE COVERAGE**
> If you carry expensive tools or supplies in your vehicle, you'll want to be sure that your commercial vehicle policy covers them. This is generally known as theft from unattended auto coverage.

## ■ Equipment theft

You may want to cover your tools and other items connected with your work at each of your job sites. Depending upon your work style, this coverage may or may not be worthwhile. As a general rule, it's better to minimize a risk than to pay extra money for insurance. If your jobs require particularly expensive equipment but you can take that equipment home with you or lock it safely at the job site, then save yourself the money and don't buy the coverage. This is a matter of personal choice, but my feeling is that insurance should be purchased for risks a contractor can't afford and not for risks that he can assume.

## ■ Nonowned auto coverage

This coverage protects your business when there is a claim that involves a vehicle other than the one that you have insured. For example, one of your employees stops at the building-supply store on the way to the job site and is involved in an accident while carrying business supplies. If there is a suit and your company is involved in it because the employee was on company business, your company would be covered for liability, although the employee would need his own liability coverage.

## ■ When insurance is required by contract

The insurance choices that I've covered to this point are for coverages that you, the contractor, need during the normal course of your business. There may be times when the customer for whom you are working has specific insurance requirements that you must meet to satisfy the contract. There are two common instances when the insurance will be dictated by the contract:

- When you are working as a subcontractor to a general contractor

- When you are working on a moderate-size commercial enterprise such as an office building

Some of these requirements are relatively easy to understand, such as requirements that you maintain general liability insurance of a certain amount and insurance related to your vehicle and your employees. Some of these provisions, however, are difficult to comprehend. For example, many contracts require that you agree to a "waiver of subrogation." I often hear comments from contractors such as "How am I supposed to know what words like 'waiver of subrogation' mean in my subcontract to do electrical work in an office building? I'm an electrician, not a lawyer!" A good insurance broker who has a lot of experience with contractors is important here. Call her and go over the terms and restrictions of the proposed contract. There are two reasons for this:

- **COMPLIANCE WITH YOUR POLICY:** Your insurance broker will be able to determine whether any provision in your contract violates your insurance policies or requires that you pay an additional premium.

- **ADEQUATE PRICING:** You'll understand what special insurance costs are involved in a particular job and thus price the job correctly.

**Q:** How do I know what insurance to buy and if I have enough coverage?

**A:** In simple terms, there are three steps:

1. Consider the risks of your particular business.

2. Talk with an independent broker who has experience with contractors.

3. Decide what risks you can afford without insurance and what risks you can't.

> **Translation Please!**
>
> Lost with the lingo? Here are a few of the common insurance terms that you'll hear:
>
> - **Subrogation:** The right of the insurance company to step into your shoes if you have a claim against another party. Giving up that right by contract may violate your insurance policy, and insurance companies often require an additional premium to permit a contractor to agree to a waiver of subrogation provision.
> - **Insured person or insured party:** The businesses and people that are covered by an insurance policy. You should be certain that all of your liability insurance policies cover your business, yourself, and all employees.
> - **Event or incident:** The specific activities for which liability insurance is provided. For example, CGL insurance should cover damages to persons or property resulting from your or your employees' negligence while performing work. Such a policy should also cover damages resulting from materials, tools, and equipment brought onto the site by you or your employees to do work.
> - **Premium:** The price of an insurance policy. Premiums may be paid annually, semiannually, quarterly, and occasionally at other times.
> - **Deductible:** The amount that you must pay for particular damage before the insurance company becomes responsible for further amounts.
> - **Exclusion:** Situations, equipment, practices, and people for whom insurance coverage is not provided by a policy.

## Insurance for Employees

Bringing on an employee can be an expensive proposition. Among the significant expenses are the insurance coverages that you provide for your employees. Some coverages are required by the state, some are optional employee benefits, and others are not mandatory but certainly necessary for proper protection of your business. Before you decide to hire an employee, find out the cost of the required coverages as well as the costs of the optional coverages. Decide which employee benefits you can afford to offer. Then decide to hire or not to hire.

> **Q:** **Do my insurance needs change if I hire an employee?**
> **A:** Yes, your insurance picture will look very different once you have an employee. You'll need to review your general liability and vehicle insurance policies to see if there are any provisions that should now be changed. In addition, you'll need:
> - Workers' compensation insurance
> - Unemployment insurance
> - Possibly medical insurance

## ■ Mandatory coverages for employees

Every state requires that employees be covered by some form of workers' compensation and some form of unemployment insurance. While the requirements vary from state to state, they aren't negotiable in any given state.

**Workers' compensation insurance**   This coverage provides compensation for employees who are unable to work because of an injury or illness that is related to their work. The amount of compensation given and the length of time the employee can collect it depend on the injury or illness sustained by the employee, the numbers of employees, the salaries paid, the particular form of work involved, and the safety record of the business.

States have different official organizations, sometimes called workers' compensation commissions, that decide what benefits the employee will receive. The laws in virtually every state specify that job-related injuries and illnesses must be handled through the workers' compensation system. Since these benefits are available, this means that in most situations the employee doesn't have the option of suing the employer.

The cost of workers' compensation insurance is also set by law in most states. That cost varies, however, depending upon such factors as the number of employees, the work hours of the employees, and the occupations of the employees. Because each state has its own formula for determining the cost of workers' compensation insurance, you really have nothing to say about it. Be clear with your broker about what activities your employees are involved in so that she can price your coverage correctly. Your broker will tell you the cost and the companies that can provide the coverage to you.

*Before you decide to hire an employee, find out the cost of the required coverages as well as the costs of the optional coverages. Decide which employee benefits you can afford to offer.*

## Workers' Compensation—A Win-Win Situation

Suppose you and your employee are putting up heavy 12-ft. joists across the ceiling of a new porch. As you reach to place your end of a joist in its joist hanger, you slip and let go of the joist and the other end falls and hits your employee's knee. He's rushed to the emergency room with a fractured kneecap and he's in a great deal of pain. A soft cast, six weeks of lost work, 20 physical therapy sessions, and a workers' compensation claim against you and your company are the results.

The workers' compensation claim is your employee's only remedy for this job-related injury: There won't be a negligence suit against you and your company. From the point of view of both parties, this works out well, since you don't want to be sued, your employee wants to get fair compensation for the job-related injury he sustained, and the two of you plan to continue to work together after he has recovered. You should certainly consult a lawyer briefly about the claim and your employee will use a workers' compensation lawyer for himself, but the issue should be resolved easily using the workers' compensation process.

If you're in business for yourself with no employees, some states provide a way for you to avoid purchasing workers' compensation insurance for yourself. Sometimes this involves using a certain type of corporation, which is fairly simple to accomplish. Even though it may be possible to avoid buying workers' compensation insurance for yourself, buy it anyway. If you have a job-related injury or illness, which may be long and expensive, your workers' compensation insurance may be the only way that your expenses will be covered.

**Unemployment insurance**   Because unemployment insurance is a state requirement, it is another matter about which you have no control. In most states, unemployment insurance is provided by the state itself or a state agency. The cost of unemployment insurance is generally based upon the earnings of the person who is insured. The broker who handles your other business insurance should also be able to handle your unemployment insurance.

*Even though it may be possible to avoid buying workers' compensation insurance for yourself, buy it anyway.*

■ Other employee insurance issues

Besides workers' compensation and unemployment insurance, there are other insurance issues to consider and discuss with your broker. These fall into the categories of liability issues and employee benefits.

**Employees and liability insurance** Be clear with your broker about what your employees do and how they work. This can have a significant impact on your basic business coverage. For example, you may want to add nonowned vehicle coverage if your employees regularly use their own vehicles as part of their job, not just to commute. Likewise, if you customarily allow your employees to drive your truck, that could affect your commercial vehicle insurance.

**Employee benefits** There are a number of types of insurance that you could consider as employee benefits. These include life, disability, and medical insurance. Other than the largest contractors, very few contractors find it possible to provide employees with life or disability insurance, and I have not found them to be necessary in any typical situations.

Medical insurance, on the other hand, is a major issue to all employees, even in the smallest businesses. Unless someone you are hiring has another source of medical insurance, such as a spouse who has family medical insurance through his or her job, the subject of medical insurance is almost surely going to be an issue when you hire an employee. There are state and federal requirements regarding equal provision of medical insurance to employees if an employer provides medical insurance. No state at present requires employers to provide and pay for medical insurance for employees. However, a few states have fairly complicated requirements regarding the provision of medical insurance to employees. Be sure to check your state requirements.

The types of medical insurance and the cost of getting it are covered in chapter 9.

## ■Including Insurance Costs in Your Prices

Your costs for insurance will probably be a big part of your budget. To run a sound and profitable business, you must make sure that all your costs are passed along to your customers—either indirectly through your hourly rate or directly by billing the cost of the insurance required for that job. Going back to some of the terminology introduced in chapter 1, insurance costs will either be a general overhead expense or a variable expense:

- **GENERAL OVERHEAD EXPENSE:** As a general rule, your insurance costs are part of your general overhead expenses. When calculating your hourly rate, you add up all your general overhead expenses. Include here all insurance policies that you maintain on an ongoing basis, such as your general liability, excess liability, commercial auto, workers' compensation, and unemployment.

- **VARIABLE EXPENSE:** If you need a specific policy or coverage for one particular job or contract, then the cost of the insurance for that job should be billed directly to that customer. Better yet, have the customer take out the policy and then you don't get involved in the cash flow. Contractors often do this with builder's risk policies. The customer who is having the house or the addition built will take out the policy and pay for it. You are covered, but they are paying for it.

## ■ Record keeping

Keep copies of all of your insurance policies, coverage descriptions, and premium notices. Some of these documents can be pretty long, particularly the policies, but it's important that you keep them and that you can find them when you need them. The product that you bought from the insurance company is an agreement to provide certain coverages. If you don't have a copy of that contract, you have no proof of what rights you have purchased. You should insist that your broker give you copies of all the insurance policies that you purchase. These should be the full policies and not summaries in the form of brochures or sales flyers.

> **TIP**
>
> **KEEPING TRACK OF YOUR POLICIES**
> Create a separate folder for each type of insurance that you purchase (general liability, excess liability, workers' compensation, and so on), and put all of the documents and correspondence related to each policy in those folders. If you should have a claim, you'll know exactly where to look for the information that you need.

## ▬Filing Claims

When you get your policies, look them over with your broker. Ask her to explain what you need to do to file a claim for each type of policy. If there are special instructions or phone numbers for making a claim, write these on the inside of your insurance folder. The last thing you need at such a time is to fumble through a pile of papers looking for the number of the claim department.

Everyone has heard stories of problems with insurance companies when settling claims. Despite the stories, this is the exception, not the rule. But you want to be prepared for the exception, just in case you are one. There are several things that you can do to help your claim be settled promptly and fairly:

*Your broker is your ally and needs to be kept informed. If there is a question or a problem with the claim, your broker can usually help untangle some of the red tape.*

- Follow all of the insurance company's procedures as best as you can.

- Keep a copy of everything that you send to the insurance company in your insurance folder—no exceptions.

- Send a copy of everything that you send to the insurance company to your broker—no exceptions. Your broker is your ally and needs to be kept informed. If there is a question or a problem with the claim, your broker can usually help untangle some of the red tape.

- If you have any conversations about the claim, such as with an insurance claims adjuster, make a note about the conversation and put that note in your insurance folder. For example, if the adjuster said that he would send you a check for $1,000, make a note something like this: "Spoke with John Doe from XYZ Insurance on May 1, 2002. He said that XYZ would pay for the tools that were stolen from the Anderson job site and that he would send me a check for $1,000 by May 8, 2002." If the check doesn't come when you expect it, you'll know whom to call and can tell him exactly what he had promised.

- Put the insured's name (normally your company's name), the policy number, the date of loss, and the claim number (once you have it) on all correspondence, notifications, accident reports, medical records, and motor vehicle reports that you send to your insurance company.

You'll receive the quickest possible response if you do these things carefully, and if there is any problem when settling the claim, you have a complete record of what happened.

# Working with an Agent or Broker

A good insurance agent or broker will discuss with you all of the forms of insurance you need to do your business and the best and most economical way to get the coverage. Select an insurance broker who is familiar with contracting businesses, who is available to answer your questions about coverages and contracts quickly and efficiently, and who can help you save money without sacrificing necessary protection.

## ■ Choosing the right broker

Take your time to choose your insurance agent or broker carefully, using the same guidelines as you did when choosing a lawyer: Interview the candidate first, ask for references, and check the references.

Make sure that the broker you choose is knowledgeable about contractors' insurance coverages. In addition to strong insurance knowledge, look for someone who can give you objective information and suggest coverages with your best interests in mind. Also ask her about the companies that she represents. Your broker should be familiar with these sources and the ratings of the companies you may be considering. It's important to deal only with companies with high ratings (AAA is best). Insurance company ratings are found in Standard & Poor's, Moody's, and A. M. Best.

## ■ Insurance company employees, agents, and brokers

There are generally three categories of salespeople who sell insurance: employees of insurance companies, agents, and brokers (independent agents).

- **EMPLOYEES:** These are people who are actually employed by an insurance company. Independence is impossible here, so don't consider this category. No one expects a GM dealer to

> **TIP**
>
> **AGENT OR BROKER?**
> There's a big difference between dealing with an agent who sells for just one insurance company and an independent broker who represents many insurance companies: You get more objective advice from a broker.

make an honest comparison between his cars and Ford's and Chrysler's.

- **AGENTS:** An agent doesn't work for a particular company as a salaried employee, but she has a regular relationship selling insurance for that company. Some agents are agents for several companies, while others are exclusive agents for one particular company. Although agents who represent several companies may be a little more independent than those who represent only one company, it is unreasonable to rely on them for independent advice. You shouldn't use an agent for the same reason that you shouldn't use an employee of an insurance company. You want total independence from the person you'll rely on to purchase your insurance, and you won't get that from an agent.

- **BROKERS (INDEPENDENT AGENTS):** These are insurance people who represent a number of insurance companies without specific allegiance to any one of them. This is your best bet. You want your broker to be able to recommend the best insurance available on the market, no matter which company may be providing it.

If you have any questions about whether a representative is an agent or an independent broker, ask her when you first talk to her.

*An insurance broker who understands the contracting business should be able, in one meeting, to review with you all of your insurance needs and the approximate costs of providing for them.*

## ■ Meeting with your broker

Once you have selected a broker, set a meeting with her and be prepared to explain everything about the type of work you do, how you do it, where you do it, the customers you serve, the equipment you own, and everything about the employees you're using. You want to be sure that your broker understands all of the possible liability issues that exist in your business, as well as issues that affect your employees. An insurance broker who understands the contracting business should be able, in one meeting, to review with you all of your insurance needs and the approximate costs of providing for them. If the person you're speaking with is not able to do this, move on and get someone else.

When you meet with your insurance broker and complete your insurance applications, answer all of the questions as thoroughly and specifically as you can. You may be tempted to save a few dollars by being less than honest on your application. For most companies, your signed application is part of the contract. If you intentionally falsify your application, your insurance company may have the right to void the contract and deny any claims. It's not only illegal but also not worth the risk.

As with other subjects in this book, such as tax matters and record keeping, I recommend that you address your insurance situation in advance of each year and sit down with your broker to go over your needs for the next year. Remember, too, if you have any change in your business that may affect your insurance, such as a new vehicle or employee changes, be sure to let your broker know. While insurance companies are pretty reasonable about their notification requirements, failure to give timely notification can be reason for a company to deny a claim.

Insurance is not a luxury; it's a necessity, whether the laws in your state say so or not. Since it is one of the larger financial investments that you make in your business, you need to be as careful with it as you would a major piece of equipment. Keep in mind that even if your insurance costs seem high, they are nothing compared with the costs of a major lawsuit.

The good news is that if you take the time to make correct decisions in the beginning, maintaining your insurance coverage doesn't require continuous attention. You can then spend your time doing what you do best and continue to improve your company's profitability. And you can do it knowing that you won't be faced with an unexpected financial disaster that could put you out of business.

*If you intentionally falsify your application, your insurance company may have the right to void the contract and deny any claims. It's not only illegal but also not worth the risk.*

# CHAPTER 9

# Medical Insurance:
## How to Live with It

One of the most important subjects workers face today is medical insurance. Medical insurance is any form of plan you purchase that provides you with either payments for medical care or medical care itself if you become ill or injured. There are a number of factors that make this a sensitive and serious issue for today's contractor:

- You and your family can't live safely without it.

- It is expensive.

- Finding good coverage and getting the most out of it can be difficult for small businesses.

The first item applies to almost anyone today, but the second and third (cost and availability) can be particularly difficult for a small contractor who owns a business. Workers who are employees of a large business typically have reasonable medical insurance benefits available to them. For the small business owner, it's not that simple. Signing up for medical insurance isn't as easy as filling out a few forms on your first day at work. Without the financial and statistical benefit of a large group to share the costs of the medical benefits, it's difficult for medical insurance companies to provide adequate and affordable coverage to individuals and small groups.

There are many things you can do to ensure that you will make the best possible selection of medical insurance from the types that are available to you and to use the medical insurance you get to its best advantage. As with other complicated issues, such as taxes, I recommend that you find a good medical insurance broker to guide you in your choice. But you need to do some legwork yourself and understand what you are buying. Don't hesitate to ask around for opinions and recommendations from your fellow contractors, your customers, and your suppliers.

In this chapter, I'll cover the various sources available to you for group medical coverage, the types of coverage plans, how to buy medical insurance, what to look for in the companies and policies, and how best to use your coverage once you have it.

# Basic Medical Coverage

Untangling what seems like almost unlimited choices and possibilities for medical coverage can be challenging. Here's a brief outline of medical coverage—what it does and what it doesn't do.

## What's usually included

All forms of medical insurance plans provide some form of payment or some form of service if you become ill or injured. Generally, these include such medical services as:

- Visits to your doctor and the treatment she recommends

- Hospital stays

- Surgery

## What's sometimes included

Medical coverage can include many other services, but there is a big difference between plans about what they will cover, how

---

**Medical Insurance Survival Checklist**

1. Check to see if you can get coverage through your spouse's employer.
2. Find out if laws in your state guarantee you the right to get certain forms of medical insurance under certain circumstances.
3. Check to see whether any labor or trade association or other group to which you belong—or which you could easily join—offers any form of medical insurance coverage to its members.
4. Learn the basic forms of medical insurance coverages available.
5. Learn the different types of medical insurance plans available.
6. Learn the major points of comparison you should use in comparing medical insurance coverages.
7. Find a knowledgeable independent agent or broker who has the time and an interest in serving you.
8. Review all of the above matters with your broker.
9. Review the available insurance coverages, particularly specific requirements such as preapproval for services.
10. If your doctor suggests that you are not eligible for a procedure that you believe is necessary, don't hesitate to question that choice.
11. If your insurance company denies coverage or reimbursement for a procedure that you feel is covered, be prepared to contest the decision. Have one or two good allies, such as your independent agent or broker or a lawyer, to help you with this.

much, how often, and so forth. Other medical care that is often paid for (in part or in total) includes prescriptions, specialist consultations, injections, various types of therapy, maternity care, home health care, outpatient surgery and care, hospice care, and medical emergency care. There are many others depending upon your plan.

### ■ Limits of liability, deductibles, copayments

Not only is there a big difference between the medical services that various plans cover but also a big difference between how much they will pay for. Typically, there is a maximum amount that an insurer will pay for each type of service as well as a maximum total that it will pay for each insured person each year (limits of liability). Some plans have deductibles (the amount that the insured person must pay before the insurer pays anything), while others have copayments or cost-sharing arrangements where the insured person pays either a fixed amount for a service or a percentage of the service.

### ■ What's often not covered

All forms of medical insurance plans are subject to limitations. Some of the more common include:

- Medical services that are not provided, such as physical therapy, cosmetic surgery, and care for mental illnesses

- Preventive visits (some plans only pay if you are sick)

- Limitations on the medical care providers you may use, such as designated doctors and hospitals

- Limitations on medical care outside the network of a provider

## ▬Group Medical Coverage

Most medical insurance policies work on the basis of belonging to a group. Since this book isn't meant to be a highly technical insurance manual, I'll explain this in simplistic and general terms, which do not cover every situation. Basically, the larger the group, the more likely it is that coverage will be affordable and less likely that the insurer will need to look closely at each person in the group. In a

**Q:** **If my employees and I are covered under workers' comp, why do I need medical coverage?**

**A:** First, workers' compensation insurance will not get you into hospitals or in to see other health care providers. Second, workers' compensation only applies to job-related illnesses and injuries—not to routine illnesses and injuries. Workers' compensation insurance is no substitute for good medical insurance coverage.

**Lost in the Lingo?**

Here's a quick explanation of some of the terms you will be hearing:

- **Copayment:** The fixed amount the insured person must pay for a particular medical service.
- **Cost share:** The amount that the insured person must pay for a covered service. This may be in the form of a copayment, a percentage of the cost, or other computation.
- **Exclusion:** A medical care cost that is not covered by a particular plan, such as physical therapy, psychiatric care, cosmetic surgery, drugs and devices, and particular medical procedures such as bone marrow transplants.
- **Gatekeeper physician:** The general physician who is assigned to members of health maintenance organizations and determines when particular procedures, drugs, specialists, tests, and so on are appropriate.
- **Insured person:** The people (you, your spouse, your children) for whom medical care is provided by an insurance plan.
- **Limits of liability:** The maximum amount the insurer will pay for the medical care of an insured person or the total medical care provided by an insurance plan.
- **Out-of-network:** Medical care that is provided by a provider not within the network of approved providers of the insurance plan.
- **Preexisting condition:** A medical condition that existed before medical insurance coverage was obtained.
- **Provider:** An individual or business that provides medical care to insured persons.

nutshell, there's safety and economy in numbers. Nearly everyone in the group is entitled to enroll in the group and will pay premiums based only on their ages and possibly where they live.

Many small contractors are not large enough to be considered a group. This can pose a problem to contractors because when you apply for insurance as an individual or as a very small group, your insurer has fewer people to include in the averages. The insurer will look at you and each person in your small group and take into consideration not only your age but also other factors that might affect your future claims, such as your occupation and medical history.

### ■ Where can I get group medical insurance?

If being part of a group is best, does that mean that the average small contractor is out of luck? No, far from it. You may be able to join other groups, such as a group through your spouse's employer, a group through a professional organization or trade association, or a group that your state makes available to you by law.

**Employer group medical insurance**  If your spouse works for an employer, public or private, that offers employees a health plan, this is probably the first place to look. If your spouse has a plan available, he or she can most likely include the entire family on the policy at an additional cost. Ask for an explanation of the benefits and options available from your spouse's employer. Since most employers pay some portion of the cost of health care coverage for their employees and a few employers even pay the total cost, this could be a good choice for you financially. This option doesn't involve your business at all; it only works if all you need to do is get coverage for yourself. If you have employees to consider, you'll need to look at one of the other options available.

*A group medical plan could be available to you from a labor or trade association to which you belong.*

**Professional or trade organization medical insurance**  Organizations that represent various groups of people often make medical and other insurance available to their members. Since organizations are like large businesses because they have more buying power than single individuals, group plans are often better than any plan you could purchase yourself. A group medical plan could be available to you from a labor or trade association to which you belong. You might belong to such an association because it represents contractors like you on a national, statewide, or even local basis or because it is useful to you in finding work. To find out about what medical coverage is available to you and what the costs are, contact the organization directly.

**Group medical insurance available by law**  Because of the difficulty that small businesses often have in getting adequate and affordable medical insurance, many states have tried to remedy this in various ways. Some states require insurance companies and other medical care providers to offer medical insurance to people who are employed in businesses that are very small. Some states even go so far as to prevent insurers from denying coverage because of such factors as past medical history, age, and where the insureds live. Insurers in these states create groups specifically for small employers that are unable to obtain insurance.

If you are a business that falls in this category and your state has this kind of law, you may take advantage of it as a means to get medical insurance for your employees. This helps to ensure that all people have the insurance that they require, regardless of whether they are directly associated with an existing group. The requirements of each state differ concerning people to whom insurance must be made available at particular prices. Discuss this with your broker or call your state's insurance commission.

---

### State Laws: Helping Out the Little Guy

Bruce, an electrician, formed an LLC a few years ago, and the business has done well. He has hired two other electricians and is planning to add a third. Bruce would like to offer medical coverage to them as an employee benefit, but he is concerned because of the size of his company.

The good news is that Bruce's business is in a state where all small businesses, from 2 to 50 employees, are pooled for medical insurance purposes. This means that any company that offers medical insurance to small businesses in Bruce's state must offer the identical medical insurance to every small business in the state. In addition, the insurance companies are only allowed to adjust their premiums based upon the ages of employees and the type of business, not on the basis of medical history or preexisting conditions. This is particularly good news since one of the employees is a recent cancer survivor. Without the special law in Bruce's state, she would be considered an extremely risky prospect, and the premium for her family would be sky-high.

---

**Small group or individual coverage**   If you can't get coverage through one of the groups listed above, you may be able to purchase either individual or small group medical coverage. This is probably your most expensive and difficult route. Your insurance broker can explain the benefits and costs of these plans.

## ▄▄▄Types of Medical Insurance Plans

Regardless of how you find your medical insurance, medical coverages are offered through four basic types of plans: unrestricted reimbursement, preferred provider, health maintenance organizations, and point-of-source.

### ■ Unrestricted reimbursement

This was the standard form of medical insurance until 15 to 20 years ago, but it is rarely available today and when it is, it is very expensive. This type of plan gives the insured the freedom to go to just

## Health Care Plans at a Glance

**Unrestricted reimbursement medical insurance**

- These are rare and usually expensive.
- You can visit the doctor, hospital, or other care provider of your choice.
- Payment rests on services and charges being "necessary and reasonable."

**Preferred provider plans**

- This is the top choice from the standpoint of quality.
- It is usually expensive.
- The plan works through a network of preferred providers, which are doctors, hospitals, and other care providers that you are allowed to use.
- Payment goes directly from the insurer to the health care provider.

**Health maintenance organizations**

- This is an economical choice.
- The quality of care is inconsistent.
- You must see an assigned primary care physician who holds the power to provide treatment and referrals.
- This is the most controversial plan.

**Point-of-source plans**

- This plan is very limiting, but it can also be very economical.
- The quality of care is inconsistent.
- You must go to an assigned facility that provides most routine services.

about any doctor or service provider he chooses, but the health care that he gets must be considered "medically necessary" and the charges "reasonable." As long as the surgery or office visit is necessary and the charges are in the range of what is considered normal, the insurer pays the bill. Of course, these policies could have exclusions or restrictions for certain medical expenses such as psychotherapy and cosmetic surgery.

## ■ Preferred provider

This is the form of medical insurance that is generally most desirable today, but, of course, it is expensive. Unlike unrestricted reimbursement, preferred provider (PPO) plans put some restrictions on which doctors and medical care providers you can use. Preferred provider medical insurance requires you to stay within the network of providers that are qualified as "preferred providers" by the insurer.

The insurer makes an agreement with each of the preferred providers (doctors, hospitals, and clinics) about how much each service will cost, then the insurer pays the preferred provider directly and usually for the full amount. With the better insurance companies, the network is very large and covers nearly all of the first-choice health care providers. If the network doesn't include a special doctor or service that you need, you will have to get approval from the insurance company to go out-of-network.

It's not unusual in average-cost states for top-of-the-line, preferred provider insurance for a couple with children to cost $1,000 per month or even more. For most contractors, this is not affordable, but as with many things, "affordable" is a matter of personal choice. The decision as to how much to spend on medical insurance is a very personal one. In making this decision, there are certain factors that you should take into account (see the sidebar below).

## ■ Health maintenance organizations

Health maintenance organizations (HMOs) are the most common and most controversial type of medical insurance today. The quality of HMOs in terms of providing medical care differs greatly. This is one area where you need to do some investigation. Talk with your broker as well as your friends and associates and learn as much as you can about the HMOs in your area.

The common factor that is found in nearly every HMO is the use of an assigned or chosen general physician for each insured person. This primary care physician is sometimes known as the gatekeeper because she determines whether patients are referred to specialists, whether they get various forms of testing, and even whether patients are told at all about various medical options.

There may be monetary or other incentives offered to the primary care physician to keep medical costs reasonable; there have been questions about some HMOs that suggest these incentives do not always work in the best interest of the patient. Since your primary care physician has a great deal of control over your medical treatment and options, it is important that you be aware of how each HMO that is available to you deals with primary care physicians and what restrictions it places on those physicians.

---

**How Important Is Medical Coverage to You?**

When you make your choice about medical plans, here are some of the factors that you need to consider:

- What can you really afford?
- What limits of liability give you the protection you feel you need in the event of serious illness or injury?
- What medical costs are you willing to pay yourself in terms of a copayment or deductible?
- Do you have special needs for particular services that some insurance plans exclude?
- Do you have a particular need for drugs or any form of medical devices?
- Do you need to have medical care available in another state?

### ■ Point-of-source

Point-of-source medical insurance requires insured persons to go to a particular place or places to get medical assistance. This can be convenient but also limiting. It generally reduces the insurer's costs, and the savings should be passed along to you. The quality of care available under a point-of-source insurance policy depends on where you get the medical care. If you're considering this option, the recommendations of your broker and the experiences of friends and coworkers can be your best guidance. If you have a special condition or illness that can't be treated at the normal facility, you will probably be referred to a different doctor or service provider for it. Find out how the plan you are considering handles these situations and where you may need to go for special medical needs.

---

**Major Medical Coverage**

For some people who are willing to take the risk of some but not the greatest medical expenses, the purchase of major medical insurance only is a possibility. If you make this choice, you must be careful to understand precisely what is considered to be "major" and what is not because you will be paying for all medical expenses of illnesses and injuries that are not major. Depending upon this definition, the medical care that will not be covered may be very substantial. For most contractors, this is an option I would not recommend, but if you feel that the costs of all other plans are simply too high for you, major medical coverage falls into the category of "something is better than nothing."

---

## ■Selecting the Right Medical Insurance

Once you are clear about the types of medical insurance coverage, you're ready to select a broker to help you find the best coverage for your money. A good broker will explain various common policy features and point out differences in the companies that sell insurance.

### ■ Using a broker

It is unlikely that the broker you use for your liability coverages will also handle medical insurance competently, so you'll probably need to find a good broker to help you with medical insurance issues. Review the information on pp. 143–144 about the types of salespeople who sell insurance. My recommendation is to find an independent broker, someone who can be objective and who is familiar with the needs of contractors. Your broker should have only one interest, which is to help you find the best and most affordable medical insurance regardless of which company sells it.

**National Association of Health Underwriters** Brokers who are members of the National Association of Health Underwriters are generally qualified in their profession, and you should be able to rely upon them to provide you with all the relevant information and guidance you'll need to make your selection. In many states, there is also a state chapter in addition to the national chapter. When you are looking and interviewing, ask the broker if she is a member before you make your choice. If you don't have a good lead to an insurance representative who will serve your purposes, you may be able to get the names of brokers in your area from either the national or your state association.

**Meeting with your broker** Once you have selected your broker, set up a time to sit down with her and go over your medical insurance needs. You should explain that you're aware of the various types of medical insurance that are available but that you need specific information regarding each of the possibilities and their costs. Your broker should be able to give you specific and detailed information about the various types of policies that she recommends and their approximate costs as well as information about the companies that she represents.

**Q:** Who should I see about purchasing medical insurance?

**A:** See an independent agent or broker, not an employee of one of the insurance companies or an agent for one or more insurance companies. Independent agents or brokers may have favorite insurers, but the deck is not loaded from the beginning, as it might be if the agent sells for only one company. Would you expect to get a good recommendation for a Chevy from a Dodge dealer?

## ■ What do I look for in a medical insurance plan?

There are a number of issues you need to consider when choosing a medical insurance plan that is right for you, your family, and your employees. These include the cost, quality, and structure of the plan, the reputation of the insurance company, out-of-network coverage, and exclusions for preexisting conditions.

**Cost vs. quality of care** The two most fundamental considerations in comparing medical insurance coverage are quality of care and cost of coverage. They are typically in opposition to each other—the better the quality of care, the higher the cost. The cost includes what you pay the insurance company for your policy premium as well as what you pay out of pocket to doctors, pharmacies, therapists, and other service providers for medical care that is not covered by your policy. You will know what your premium costs are right up front. Make sure that you understand what costs you will have to cover yourself. If a certain procedure is not covered, your

*Your broker should have only one interest, which is to help you find the best and most affordable medical insurance regardless of which company sells it.*

---

**Comparing Health Care Coverage**

Confused by all of the options? Here are some of the major factors:

- Reputation of the insurers you're considering
- Cost of insurance
- Services that are limited or not covered
- General structure of health care provided by the different possible providers
- How each of the insurers you're considering deals with out-of-network health care providers
- Nature of the medical care you'll be receiving from each insurer

---

premium may be lower, but you'll need to pay for that procedure yourself.

Balancing cost versus quality is a very personal choice. What's best for one person is not necessarily best for another. For example, a healthy family with children may place a very high value on benefits such as annual physical examinations and eye care. A family with a chronically ill member may place a particularly high value on the medical care that is provided for that particular individual's illness. A family with special needs for drugs or psychiatric care will want to carefully consider the health care provided in those areas.

When comparing possible insurance plans, consider what each plan provides in your and your family's particular circumstances as well as the reputation of the insurer and the plan. Here are some of the factors that you should consider when deciding what your true cost is:

- **PRESCRIPTION DRUGS:** Check to see what the plan pays for prescriptions. If you or someone in your family has a chronic illness, this can be a huge financial burden.

- **UNCOVERED OR PARTIALLY COVERED SERVICES:** There are a number of common services that are frequently not covered by various providers.

---

**Q: If I buy good medical insurance, will it pay for everything?**

**A:** No, probably not. Even a good policy will have a deductible or a copayment for the services that it does cover. In addition, you may have to pay some or all of the expenses for:

- Medical services beyond the scope of your insurance policy
- Out-of-network situations
- Services such as physical therapy, cosmetic surgery, psychiatric and psychological counseling, home health-aide assistance, drugs, and others
- Medical assistance that your insurer does not consider to be "medically necessary," unless you're able to take steps to prove your need for it

These include routine physicals, physical therapy, cosmetic surgery, psychiatric or psychological counseling, and home health-aide assistance. Many insurers do offer some coverage for these but place strict limits on them in the various policies. If you need physical therapy at least once per week for a year and your insurance policy provides for a maximum of 10 sessions per year, you'll wind up paying for 40 or so physical therapy sessions, which can run into hundreds of dollars each.

> ### Weighing What's Important
>
> Harry, an excavation contractor, is the only employee of his own corporation and needs medical insurance coverage for himself, his wife, and two young children. Everyone in Harry's family is healthy at the present time, but Harry doesn't want to take any chances.
>
> One HMO provides what is considered to be the best HMO care available in Harry's state, but the annual premium for Harry's family would run about $7,400 compared with $5,700 for each of two other HMOs. Each of the HMOs has high limits of liability and low copay requirements, but only the expensive HMO provides for full annual medical exams and physical therapy. Harry figures the annual exams for each of the four members of his family are worth around $600, and he is likely to need physical therapy because of recurrent back problems related to work.
>
> After weighing the costs and benefits, Harry goes with the expensive HMO. The annual exams and physical therapy bring its cost to within $700 of the others, and the higher quality of its care is worth the difference. Plus, he knows that he's not stuck with his choice for the rest of his life; next year, he could change to one of the other plans.

- **MAXIMUM LIMIT OF COVERAGE:** Your best choice is a policy that has no limit to the medical coverage. However, it is pretty rare these days to find such a policy and if you do, the cost may be prohibitive. In any event, your total limit of coverage should never be less than $1 million per person.

When most contractors balance quality of care with cost, they generally choose an HMO or point-of-source insurer.

**Structure of the insurance plan**   An important consideration for you to review with your independent agent or broker is the general structure of health care offered by the different possible providers. You should be asking such questions as:

- What type of plan is this? HMO, PPO, point-of-source, other?

- If it's an HMO, find out what your choices are in selecting your primary care physician and how the gatekeeper rules work.

- If it's point-of-source, where is the facility and how is it staffed?

**Reputation of the insurance company**  What kind of reputation does the insurer have? Check with your broker for her opinion and also ask people who have bought health care coverage from various providers about their experiences, both when they have been in good health and when they have had serious illnesses.

---

**Out-of-Network and Out of Luck**

Jim, an independent drywall contractor, had finally blocked out a week during the summer to go on vacation with his family. While biking, he spun out and ended up in the emergency room of a local hospital with a broken leg. A member of the hospital business office didn't say anything when Jim gave her his insurance card and didn't ask him to pay a thing that day. He thought everything was fine—except no more biking on his vacation.

Unfortunately, he didn't read the back of his insurance card. His insurer covers out-of-network emergency services, but it requires notification to a toll-free number within 24 hours of the treatment. A month later, when Jim got the bill for $1,200 from the emergency room, his insurer denied the claim. He was out of luck and had to pay the whole bill.

---

**Out-of-network coverage**  Another important consideration is how each of the possible insurers you're considering deals with out-of-network health care providers. An out-of-network provider is a doctor, hospital, or other service provider that you use when the medical service that you need is not offered by the health care providers that are associated with your medical insurance plan. This situation can happen when you have a condition that requires a specialist, when you have an emergency that requires immediate attention, or when you are traveling.

You should discuss with your independent agent or broker how each insurer handles these situations and, in particular, whether there are preapproval requirements that might be very difficult to meet. If there are preapproval requirements, it's essential that you understand how they work and exactly what you need to do, otherwise, your medical expenses may not be paid for.

**Exclusions for preexisting conditions**  One of the most significant concerns regarding medical insurance coverage is how the coverage you are considering deals with preexisting conditions. These are illnesses or injuries that existed before you purchased the insurance. For example, if you have had chronic emphysema for five years and require daily medication and routine and ongoing therapy, this would be a preexisting condition. These situations don't necessarily present a problem, although there may be a higher premium. In some situations, however, your medical insurance policy could exclude medical treatment for these preexisting conditions, especially if it appears that you intentionally hid information about these conditions when you applied for insurance.

Generally, insurance companies learn about your present and past health when you fill out the application. Some insurers also require a physical exam or a screening. In some states, there are laws that limit the ways an insurance company can deal with a preexisting condition. In any event, to help avoid a situation where you might be denied coverage because of a preexisting condition, you should always do the following:

- Discuss the preexisting illness provisions of the insurance plan that you are considering with your broker. Have her fully explain how your plan handles this situation and also what obligations you have so that there are no surprises later.

- Answer your medical insurance application as fully and specifically as you can. If you are not sure whether a certain medical condition is considered preexisting, ask your broker. Any attempt on your part to hide a major medical condition could be a valid reason for denying coverage.

## ▬Medical Insurance and Taxes

The money that you spend on your medical insurance premiums may be deductible from your taxable income. As with other tax matters, I recommend that you check with your accountant because tax laws do change. As always, your job is to provide your accountant with complete information and copies of relevant documentation so that you will receive the maximum tax benefit you're entitled to based upon the premiums you're paying and the current law regarding your particular business. That said, here are a few general tax rules depending on the form of business you use:

- **"C" CORPORATIONS:**    When a standard corporation, known as a "C" corporation, provides medical insurance for its employees, it is possible to deduct the employer's portion of the medical insurance costs for its employees from the corporation's income and, at the same time, not charge the employees of the corporation with taxable income for the amount that

*The money that you spend on your medical insurance premiums may be deductible from your taxable income.*

the corporation pays. In addition, medical insurance need not be provided evenly to every employee of a corporation. It's possible, therefore, for the costliest medical insurance to be provided to some employees and less expensive medical insurance to others. It's even possible for a corporation to provide medical insurance to some employees but not others.

- **"S" CORPORATIONS, PARTNERSHIPS, SOLE PROPRIETORS:**
  For these types of businesses, the rules for deductions and for charging income to employees are more complicated. Present laws allow such a business to deduct a certain portion of the cost of medical insurance and to charge the employee with taxable income equal to some portion of the medical insurance premium that has been paid for that employee. The upshot of this is that for "S" corporations, partnerships, and single individuals, the deductibility and the taxability of medical insurance premiums involve complications that can't be addressed without the help of your accountant.

## Making the Best Use of Your Health Care Coverage

Once you have made your choice and you are covered under the plan that you selected, you will want to get the most out of your coverage, get treatment quickly when you need it, and be able to work with your provider. Here are some of the issues that may come up:

### ■ Policies and insurance cards

Once you get your new policy, do the following:

- Go over the policy and any special requirements with your broker. Be clear about which doctors you can use, what services are restricted, and any other special requirements.

- Write down the names and phone numbers of people you need to call for preapproval and put them in your Rolodex and in the front of your medical insurance file.

- Put your policy and all information related to it in a folder labeled medical insurance.

- Carry your insurance card with you at all times. This goes for every adult and every child who is traveling independently or attending school away from home.

- If this is a group policy that includes your employees, go over the benefits and restrictions of the coverage with all of your employees. Your employees should receive their insurance policies and cards directly from the insurer.

**Medical insurance and overhead**   It is preferable to treat the cost of medical insurance as part of general overhead, even though medical insurance is really a form of compensation and the benefits will often run to family members who are not employees of the business. Review pp. 7–12 for information about figuring your hourly rate, and be sure that you include your costs for medical insurance in that rate.

## ■ Getting routine medical help

You've got your policy and you've got your insurance card. Getting routine medical help should be just a matter of understanding how your plan works and following the instructions. Each insurer has certain requirements about how you get medical care. There may be certain doctors, hospitals, and facilities that you must use when you are sick or injured. Preapproval is necessary in some instances. In other situations, certain health care providers, most often your primary care physicians, are required to do certain things in order for the medical care to be provided to you. These include making referrals or prescriptions for the service or medicine involved.

Without the correct referral or prescription, your medical care may not be covered. For example, anyone can buy or rent a wheelchair without a note from your doctor. But to get reimbursement for it from your insurer, you generally need to have a prescription from your doctor stating that you need the wheelchair. In some instances, various forms of documentation, such as letters concerning injuries or absence from work, may be required.

> **TIP**
>
> **PERIODIC COVERAGE REVIEW**
> Insurance issues and regulations change frequently. So can your personal situation. Plan to meet with your broker every few years to go over your policy to be sure that it's up to date.

### ■ Who pays the doctor?

Various insurers differ about who pays the bills. For health care providers that are approved and in the network of a particular insurer, the general rule is that the insurer pays the provider. The insured person (you or your family member) may never even see the bill. For out-of-network services, however, there is no rule. Assuming that the service is covered by your insurance, the insurer may or may not pay the out-of-network health care provider directly. In some instances, you pay the bill and then submit the paid bill to your insurance company for reimbursement to you.

Whatever the payment arrangements may be, you'll realize the best value from your medical insurance coverage if you understand those arrangements and do whatever is necessary to satisfy them. It may seem like unnecessary paperwork, but if you want to get reimbursed quickly and fully, you'll need to do it.

### ■ Serious illnesses

Nearly every insurer has a special procedure for dealing with major illnesses and injuries. Sometimes these situations are called "catastrophic" illnesses or injuries. Whatever they are called, it's an illness or injury that seriously threatens the quality of a person's life or is life-threatening. The costs of treatment of major illnesses or injuries are very high and, of course, very worrisome to everyone.

Insurers often assign special caseworkers on their staffs to deal with catastrophic illnesses. If you are in this situation, find out who that person is and get to know her as soon and as well as you can. If it is at all possible, deal directly with that person and have her make a visit to your home. There are two main benefits:

- You will be dealing with the person who is most knowledgeable and influential in matters relating to your individual situation.

- As you work with your catastrophic caseworker, she gets to know you as a person—not just a case number. Once she gets to know you and learns about how severely this medical situation is affecting your life and the lives of your family members, she'll tend naturally to become sympathetic. As she better understands your needs and your circumstances, she will be in a better position to help you get faster action and hopefully fuller payment.

## ■ If coverage is declined

If your insurer declines to pay for medical care that is excluded from coverage by your policy, there is probably nothing you can do about that. However, if your insurer declines medical care that may be covered but makes the argument that such care is not "medically necessary," you'll have a fight on your hands, but it is sometimes a fight that you can win. If your doctor or insurance company tells you that you shouldn't get a treatment that you feel you need, you have the right to question that decision. There are various ways for you to show that particular care is medically necessary. Your independent agent or broker and sometimes a lawyer may assist you in such a matter.

Besides understanding the conditions you must meet to obtain insurance coverage and understanding how to go to the mat with your insurer when it denies coverage that you may be entitled to, there are other fine points in dealing with medical coverage providers that depend upon particular circumstances. This is one of those areas where it is often worth spending a little money on a lawyer's or accountant's fee to get the best available advice. If you do this, be sure to present to her a precise outline of your problem. This should include your insurance policy, a detailed description of the health care that is in dispute, and a chronological review of all steps you have taken with regard to the particular matter.

Understanding and getting good health care coverage can be very difficult, but it is extremely important. It is worth taking the time to understand the basic concepts and your many choices, but you don't have to do this alone. Use the help that is readily available to you. Talk with other contractors, your friends, your customers, and your suppliers to find out what worked and didn't work for them. And get yourself a good independent broker to help you with your choice. Good working knowledge, a capable independent agent or broker, and clear thinking will get you through the matter of medical insurance.

*If your doctor or insurance company tells you that you shouldn't get a treatment that you feel you need, you have the right to question that decision.*

# CHAPTER 10

# Disability:
## Anticipating the Solution

*In most forms of physical work that involve pulling and pushing of muscles and joints, the question is not whether you will become disabled but when.*

Unlike many professions where disability is little more than a remote possibility, the nature of the work that many contractors do makes disability a very real threat. Disability can be one of the worst financial and personal situations any contractor can experience. There are a number of reasons why:

- **REDUCED INCOME:** Disability, by definition, ends or limits your ability to do some or all of your work. Total disability ends your work altogether. Partial disability permits you to do some of your work but most likely with difficulty.

- **INCREASED EXPENSES**: Disabilities are generally accompanied by considerable costs including medical care, devices and machines that assist with the disability, and sometimes expenses for the assistance of other persons.

- **UNPREDICTABILITY:** You could become disabled tomorrow, in 20 years, or, hopefully, never. Likewise, your disability could last for a few months, a year, a decade, or a lifetime.

- **UNCERTAIN FUTURE:** With a disability, life as you know it changes. That change can be temporary or permanent. Not only is your income reduced and your expenses increased, but also you may not know if or when your life will return to "normal."

# Disability: A Clear and Present Danger

In most forms of physical work that involve pulling and pushing of muscles and joints, the question is not whether you will become disabled but when. This is especially true for contractors who rely heavily on particular sets of muscles and joints to do their work, very often exerting and stressing themselves beyond the point of endurance. This occurs more often and earlier in particular trades, such as frame carpentry, but even in trades where your body is not put in a difficult position for long periods of time, the normal decline of strength, coordination, and endurance eventually takes its toll. Because of the high probability of becoming disabled, it's essential that contractors make plans for that possibility. In this chapter, I will discuss total and partial disabilities and how to deal with those possibilities through insurance and other methods.

# Disability Insurance

A good disability insurance policy is a first step in planning a solution for disability. This type of policy pays you certain amounts on a regular basis after an exclusion period (typically three to six months). Many policies state that if you're unable to do three-quarters of your regular work, you will be considered totally disabled and entitled to full payments. Disability payments are normally made monthly and continue for periods of disability of different lengths. A typical policy will call for payments until you are 65 years of age.

Getting good disability coverage is not an easy task. There are a couple of reasons why:

- **COST:** The price of any disability insurance that is worth having is quite high.

- **RESTRICTIONS IN BENEFITS:** Disability insurance policies have in recent years become more restrictive about the definition of "disability" and more demanding about what you must do to be eligible for disability payments.

Understanding how disability insurance works and having a good broker to help you will improve your chances of getting adequate and affordable coverage.

> **TIP**
>
> **GET A GOOD BROKER**
> When looking for insurance, your first step is to find an independent agent or broker who has a good working knowledge of disability insurance and the policies available. This person should also be knowledgeable about the contracting business (see chapter 8 for guidelines for finding a good broker).

## ■ Disability insurance issues to consider

When you discuss disability insurance with your broker, there are a number of issues you should take into account. These include:

- Availability of coverage

- Period of contestability

- Full disclosure

- Loss of "own occupation" coverage

- Disability definition and collecting benefits

- Exclusion period

- How much disability insurance to buy

- Guaranteed renewability

- Long-term vs. short-term policies

- Total vs. partial disability

- Insurance company ratings

**Availability of coverage** If you are already showing signs of a disability or have a condition that predisposes you to it, there is almost no chance that any credible insurance company will provide you with a disability insurance policy of any value to you. Medical underwriting is particularly strict for disability insurance coverages. Therefore, you should buy your disability insurance early in your career. If you were not able to do that and find that you are not eligible for

---

### The Language of Disability

Confused by the language? Here are a few definitions:

- **Total disability:** The loss of your ability to do all of your work.
- **Partial disability:** The loss of your ability to do some but not all of your work.
- **Own occupation disability insurance:** Disability insurance that provides you with payments if you are unable to perform some or all of the duties of your regular occupation.
- **Exclusion period:** The period of time during which you must be disabled before you are entitled to disability payments.
- **Guaranteed renewability:** A provision in a disability insurance policy that assures you of the right to purchase disability insurance in future years at established premiums. Ten years is typical in disability insurance policies.
- **Period of contestability:** The period of time within which the insurance company may contest your right to disability payments by asserting that you provided inaccurate medical or other information. Two years is typical in disability insurance policies.
- **Waiver of premium:** A provision in a disability insurance policy that excuses you from paying future premiums if you become disabled.

disability coverage, there are other ways in which you can prepare for a possible disability (see "Other Solutions for Dealing with Disability" on pp. 172–177).

**Period of contestability**   Until what is known as the "period of contestability" expires, disability insurance companies reserve the right to challenge any claim for coverage based upon a finding that any representation made by the insured person is false. Periods of contestability are typically two years, but they are sometimes longer or shorter, so ask your broker about your policy. When a policy's period of contestability expires, coverage becomes incontestable, meaning the insurer can no longer argue about the truth or falsity of your representations to it.

**Full disclosure**   In most situations, you will be required to take a physical examination and answer a medical history questionnaire. In a few instances, the questionnaire along with a note from your own doctor may be sufficient. The information that you provide normally becomes part of the terms of the contract.

**Loss of "own occupation" coverage**   At one time, a considerable number of insurance companies offered what is known as "own occupation" disability insurance coverage. This type of coverage will pay you certain amounts after an exclusion period (typically three to six months) based upon how much of your regular work you are unable to do.

Unfortunately, own occupation disability insurance is rarely available today. Now, most disability insurance is based upon the percentage of your income that you lose due to a disability. If you are able to work in another type of job (not your "own occu-

**TIP**

**KEEP IT HONEST**
Never make a false statement about your health (or anything else) on an insurance application. You could lose your rights to coverage and even be charged with a crime.

**Read the Fine Print**

Zack, a carpenter, lost the use of his right arm in a serious automobile accident. As a result, Zack has made a claim under his own occupation disability insurance policy that he purchased two years ago.

Unfortunately, Zack's own occupation disability insurance policy is more complicated than he thought. Zack discovered when he read his policy carefully after the car accident that it requires him to be unable to do alternative work, even with training, for him to receive disability payments.

Zack's disability insurance company is arguing that since Zack is an intelligent high school graduate with full mental and physical abilities except for the use of one arm, there are many jobs Zack could be trained to do that would replace his lost income of approximately $45,000 per year. The insurance company is not arguing that Zack isn't totally disabled to continue his work as a carpenter, but it is saying that his disability is not sufficient under the policy for him to get payments. Zack has a fight ahead with the insurance company.

pation"), in some cases even if you need training to learn it, you may not be considered disabled and therefore not eligible for disability benefits. Go over this carefully with your broker. Make sure that the disability policy covers situations that really apply to you.

**Disability definition and collecting benefits**   When you speak with your broker, ask about the specific requirements dealing with definition of disability and collecting benefits. If these two areas don't work in your situation, you'll be paying a lot of money for a disability policy that you can't use. If you buy a disability insurance policy, it must be one that takes a realistic view of what will make you truly disabled in light of your work abilities. The policy must also be one that does not place ridiculous requirements in the way of collecting disability payments in the event that you are unable to work. If a policy doesn't meet these requirements, it is worthless.

**Exclusion period**   The exclusion period is the time during which you have to be disabled before disability insurance payments begin. This is typically three to six months, although it can be shorter or longer. If your particular situation would entitle you to unemployment insurance for some period of time if your loss of work was due to disability, you will probably want to take this into account in considering the exclusion period. As a general rule, the longer the exclusion period, the less expensive the premium.

*As a general rule, the longer the exclusion period, the less expensive the premium.*

**How much disability insurance to buy**   Legal requirements and the insurance companies themselves place limits on the amount of disability insurance you may purchase. These limits are usually less than the maximum earnings a person has made in recent years. If your best year in the last five wound up with your having a taxable income of $58,000, you would not be able to purchase disability insurance equal to or greater than that amount.

In most cases, however, contractors have no desire to purchase more disability insurance than is necessary to sustain their incomes. When contractors and others purchase disability insurance, it is normally for an amount substantially smaller than the best incomes they have made in recent years. Since disability insurance is a very expensive form of insurance, my recommendation is to purchase as little as possible but enough to provide you with a livable income if you should ever need it.

### How Much Coverage Should You Buy?

Russ is a 36-year-old roofer who is in reasonably good physical condition and able to purchase disability insurance at this time. He knows, however, that any significant medical problem, not to mention his 40th birthday not so far in the future, will make it nearly impossible for him to purchase disability insurance at a reasonable cost.

Russ has been looking at disability insurance along with other income sources to help him if he should become disabled. The problem now is that the other pieces of his disability plan (savings and investments) are not yet large enough for him to live adequately. Together with his other income, Russ would need about $2,500 per month tax-free disability payments to equal his present income if he becomes disabled. The cost of that much disability insurance is too high.

Russ has decided to buy a policy that would pay him $2,000 per month—and it is guaranteed renewable for 10 years. This is a good compromise. He is stretching to buy all the disability insurance he can afford now and hopes that he will not need it before the other pieces of his disability/retirement plan have grown large enough to support him adequately.

**Guaranteed renewability**   Since a claim for total or even partial disability benefits generally limits or ends your ability to buy additional insurance, purchase your disability insurance before you are disabled. Be sure that it is guaranteed renewable at a stated price for a fixed number of years. As you grow older, particularly if your health situation deteriorates, it won't be possible to purchase similar disability insurance at the same price or any reasonable price. To be really useful, guaranteed renewability at stated prices should be offered for at least 10 years.

*Since a claim for disability benefits generally limits or ends your ability to buy additional insurance, purchase your disability insurance before you are disabled.*

**Long-term vs. short-term policies**   The time for which disability payments may continue, which varies but often goes to age 65, is another important consideration in purchasing disability insurance. Long-term and short-term disability policies are available. Since contractors experience both temporary and permanent disabilities, the policy must provide coverage for a sufficiently long period to account for both. Most policies don't provide for increases in monthly pay-

> **Take Time to Compare**
>
> When shopping for your disability insurance, compare these provisions. They can have a big impact on the benefits that you may collect.
>
> - Definition of "disability" (policy should cover both total and partial disability)
> - Conditions that must be met to receive disability payments (i.e., pursuit of other work, retraining)
> - Cost and various amounts of insurance you can purchase
> - Exclusionary period
> - Period of time before incontestability
> - Time for which disability payments continue (most long-term policies pay until age 65)
> - Limit on other income you can earn while collecting disability payments (probably not own occupation)
> - Guaranteed renewability
> - Financial rating of insurance company (check with A. M. Best Company or Standard & Poor's)

ments after a disability claim is made. Therefore, you must take into account that you may be receiving a fixed payment for years in the future. This will affect your plans for retirement and possibly your estate plans (see chapter 11).

**Total vs. partial disability**   Every disability insurance policy makes a provision for partial disability as well for as total disability. Partial disability payments are typically in proportion to the amount of work ability you have lost. For example, if you lose the ability to do one-half of the work you previously did, you will receive one-half of the total disability payments. Most policies consider you totally disabled if you are disabled beyond a certain percentage, usually 75%.

**Insurance company ratings**   Finally, look for an insurance company that is sound. Since your disability payments may go on for years, you want to be sure that the company will be around to pay them. Use only insurance companies that are rated AAA by A. M. Best Company or Standard & Poor's. Your insurance agent or broker should be able to tell you about the ratings of different insurance companies.

## ■ Tax consequences of disability insurance

When choosing a disability insurance policy, consider the tax implications. The rules are based on whether you are paying the premiums yourself or whether your employer pays the premiums for you. As a general rule, if you pay for disability insurance out of your personal income after taxes have been deducted, you don't have to pay taxes on the disability insurance payments you may receive in the future.

While there are many factors to consider, it's usually best for contractors to pay for disability insurance out of their after-tax income. If you become disabled, your disability payments will not be taxed and you will have the full benefit of those payments. Since this is an important decision and depends upon various considerations that are somewhat complex, it's something you should definitely review with your accountant. Whatever decision you reach will affect the amount of disability insurance coverage you should buy.

*If you pay for disability insurance out of your personal income after taxes have been deducted, you don't have to pay taxes on the disability insurance payments you may receive in the future.*

## ■ Periodic policy review

Once you have your disability policy, keep it in your disability insurance folder. I recommend that you review the limits and benefits of your policy every few years. If your income increases significantly, you may want to increase your coverage. Since your disability insurance is only one part of the plan, you may want to make adjustments based on the values in other accounts, such as your savings, investments, and retirement.

### Ask Your Accountant...

- Should you or a business you're working for buy disability insurance for you? If you are the one buying the disability insurance, ask if you should pay disability insurance premiums with before-tax or after-tax funds.
- Is your business able to deduct disability insurance premiums as an expense of doing business?

## ■ Filing claims

Most disability insurance policies provide for payments monthly once a disability has been established, you have satisfied the conditions for collecting insurance, and the exclusionary period has expired. The sooner you begin the filing process, the sooner you will receive payments.

### ▎TIP

**FILING CLAIMS**

If you become disabled and need to make a claim for disability payments, there are two things that you can do to help your claim go smoothly: First, file promptly, and second, furnish all requested information.

To make your claim as effectively as possible, follow the insurance company's filing requirements exactly and provide all the information and documentation requested. Generally, insurance companies require medical evidence from your doctor of your illness or injury and evidence from your employer of your loss of income. If you are self-employed, your accountant should furnish the loss-of-income information because it's best that this information come from an official source. Keep a full set of copies of all of the documents in your disability insurance file folder.

## Other Solutions for Dealing with Disability

Because of the limitations and high price of disability insurance, you should also consider other ways to deal with the possibility of becoming disabled. Even if you get disability insurance that will provide you with some of the income you'll need, you should still make plans for additional means of support. A good plan for dealing with possible disability includes a number of pieces—disability insurance is just one of them. Together they will make it possible for you and your family to enjoy a reasonable lifestyle if disability overtakes you. These additional pieces include Social Security and Medicare, private benefits programs, savings and investments, retirement plans, and income from other work.

### ■ Social Security

In addition to retirement income (see chapter 11), the Social Security Administration (SSA) provides benefits to people who have disabilities. Disability benefits depend upon a number of factors, including your ability to establish that you are disabled within the meaning of the Social Security laws.

**Eligibility requirements**   The requirements for establishing a disability that would entitle you to Social Security are strict. There are two key components to the SSA's definition of a disability:

- You can't do the work you did before the disability, and you can't adjust to other work because of your condition.

- The condition must last for at least a year in order for you to receive benefits.

It is sometimes possible to get disability benefits by showing that a disability is expected to last for more than a year, but this is difficult. Even if your situation fits the definition of disability for Social Security purposes, a great deal of information and records about your medical condition and about your previous work are required to support your claim.

**Income limits** The SSA places limits on the income that you can earn. Since the definition of disability for Social Security purposes includes a requirement that you be unable to do alternative work as well as your traditional work, you will in most instances not be entitled to Social Security disability income and you won't have to worry about whether that income will be reduced if you discover a way to earn more than the allowed amounts.

The amounts allowed for earned income when you are collecting Social Security disability benefits are different from the amounts you are allowed to earn if you receive regular retirement benefits from Social Security. The SSA has fairly complicated rules for determining what you are allowed to earn if you receive disability payments, and you will need to confer directly with the SSA if that situation arises.

> **TIP**
>
> **PREPARING A CLAIM**
> Social Security disability claims can be tough. If you need to file for disability benefits, get some good coaching from a lawyer who handles Social Security claims. It will be well worth the investment.

## ■ Other benefit programs

In addition to Social Security, check to see if any program in which you have been involved entitles you to any form of disability benefits. These could include:

- Unions or trade associations

- Business and fraternal organizations to which you may belong

- Life insurance policies, which sometimes provide some form of disability benefits, although these are usually limited to major occurrences such as loss of an eye or limb

> **Medicare**
> Medicare provides a limited amount of health insurance for many but not all people with disabilities. The SSA will provide information about your eligibility. Since you will need medical insurance even more if you're disabled, it's important to know whether you will be entitled to receive Medicare at different times in the future. If you are, you should consider buying a private insurance Medicare supplement policy. These policies are reasonably priced, and your agent or broker can give you specific information about them.

Although these types of disability benefits are not common, be thorough and check them out. It could make a big difference to you financially.

## ■ Savings and investments

I'll discuss the need for savings and investments as part of an overall retirement program in chapter 11, but you should also consider savings and investments as a part of a disability plan. If your disability program depends in part upon savings and investments, you must be reasonably certain that you are putting your money in places that are relatively secure. If the total amount of your savings and investments falls substantially, the portion of your annual income that depends upon these things will be significantly reduced.

Because you have some ability to plan for retirement but disability may occur unexpectedly at any time, the forms of investment that are reasonably safe if you can leave the funds untouched for years (such as the stock market) may be perfectly sensible for retirement purposes but not so for disability purposes.

If you can find an investment advisor who is competent and interested in working with someone with the amount of funds you're putting aside, that assistance could be very useful. Unfortunately, this is often not possible. If you decide to place some of your money in such things as stocks and bonds, you'll need to take the time to learn something about those forms of investments. (A good deal of such information can be acquired from periodicals and newspapers and by using the Internet.) Until you feel you have a reasonable working knowledge of any form of investment that interests you, stay away from it. Even in what appear to be boom times, lots of investors lose a good deal of their money.

---

**Pieces of the Disability Package: Sources of Income**

- Disability insurance payments
- Social Security and Medicare
- Disability benefits from unions, trade associations, or business organizations to which you belong
- Savings and investment income
- Retirement plan income
- Workers' compensation
- Unemployment insurance
- Damage awards from another person or company if the disability results from an accident or wrongful conduct by others
- Other forms of work, including home-based businesses and working as a consultant, expert, instructor, estimator, or supervisor

## ■ Retirement plans

When you select a retirement plan that suits your needs and abilities, you'll want to consider various possibilities for your plan that may be useful to you and won't destroy the significant tax advantages of using such plans. One of these possibilities is disability. Many retirement plans contain a provision providing a person who receives the plan's benefits with the right to begin receiving payments from the plan if he should become disabled before the retirement age that is established.

Although you will have a smaller amount of money in your plan if you become disabled before the age when you planned to retire, it is still useful for you to make it possible to withdraw money from your plan in the event you become disabled. This is a matter you should discuss with the advisor who helps you establish your plan.

The same tradeoff between safety and a greater possible return exists with respect to money in your retirement plan as in your personal savings and investments. Since money in a retirement plan is generally invested for a long time and deferred taxation of earnings is one of the main features of such plans, you may not want to completely eliminate short-term risks in investing money in your plan. That is because in the long run you would almost surely reduce the earnings that are possible in the plan. You will have to make a decision that balances these concerns. When making this decision, consider your age, the age you have established for your retirement, and your best estimate of when or if you will become disabled.

*The same tradeoff between safety and a greater possible return exists with respect to money in your retirement plan as in your personal savings and investments.*

## ■ Income from other forms of work

Disability doesn't have to mean the end of your working life: You have the ability to earn significant income even if you become unable to perform your work as a contractor. You can use your knowledge and experience in your trade and continue to work on a limited basis, or you can branch out in a number of new

> **TIP**
>
> **DISABILITY PAYMENTS AND OTHER INCOME**
> Before you decide to find alternative work, consider how that income may affect your disability insurance payments. Your income could reduce your disability payments—sometimes substantially. If that happens, you may be working for nothing. Carefully review your disability insurance policy (getting help if you need it) to be certain that alternative work won't reduce any disability insurance payments you may be receiving.

directions, including consulting, estimating, supervising, or establishing a home-based business.

**Consulting—more brain, less brawn** During the course of your career, you have gained much knowledge and experience about your trade and the construction business. If you become physically disabled, you can still use that wealth of information. One way to do this is by being available as a consultant or expert in your particular trade. Various people require these consultants on a regular basis. For example, lawyers use experts in skilled trades to assist them in resolving disputes and even to testify in depositions or court trials. To find out more about consulting opportunities in your area, contact the Technical Advisory Service for Attorneys (TASA).

---

**TIP**

**WORKING AS AN ESTIMATOR**

There are a limited number of full-time positions available as estimators in various trades. If you're disabled, however, you may be more comfortable by working part time, which will earn you a smaller income but will provide a piece of the total disability package you are putting together.

---

**Estimating** Another possibility for using your expertise without doing physical work is to work as an estimator. Estimators are hired by companies for various reasons. Sometimes they are hired because a company wants to verify the cost of particular work to be able to bid on a job. Sometimes estimators are hired when it's necessary to determine the likely time and materials cost of a job.

Estimators are also hired by surety companies and others when it is necessary for a "takeover contractor" to be hired to finish a job. A takeover contractor is a contractor who finishes a job that was started by another contractor who is unable or unwilling to finish it. When the performance of a job is bonded, as is often the case in large jobs and public jobs, the surety company often needs to hire a takeover contractor.

**Supervising** Some large companies hire contractors to perform supervisory functions only. Depending upon the nature of your disability, this may be a possibility. There is also a small market for contractors who are willing to assist in publications that concern their trades.

**Starting a home-based business**   There are dozens of possibilities for work out of your home. Many of these involve the use of the Internet in one way or another, and some are jobs that pay only on a commission basis for sales of a product or service. But there are many other possibilities as well, and it may be worth your while to begin exploring them now.

You may already have an idea about what homebound work you could do if you became disabled. Some contractors start such work while they are continuing to work full time in their trades. Although this is difficult in terms of your available time, it's useful to give serious thought to this possibility and even to explore the costs and possible financial rewards of a few of the home-based businesses that seem to be appropriate for you. You may earn less in this form of work than you're earning as a contractor, but remember that we are talking about pieces of a disability/retirement program that fit together to give you a workable income.

When putting together the pieces to prepare for disability, you may find that your total income will be satisfactory for your and your family's needs. The secret to making this happen is that age-old saying "plan ahead."

Remember that there is a wide range of possibilities when you consider a disability. You may become disabled tomorrow or in 20 years. Your disability may be total or partial. The extra expenses you must bear on account of a disability vary widely. And it's even possible, if your disability results from an accident or wrongful conduct by others, that you may be able to receive an amount of workers' compensation or money damages from another person or company.

In light of these uncertainties, the best you can do is put the pieces together so that you will receive a reasonable income from all sources combined if and when you need it. I will discuss in chapter 11 how to use similar planning to provide for your retirement or semiretirement.

# Retirement Planning:
## Never Too Early

We all know that we should plan for our retirements, but the truth is that many contractors (and other workers) are simply not prepared for retirement when it comes. For some, it may be due in part to the fact that they are self-employed and aren't aware of or don't have access to the retirement plans that are available in other professions. For others, it may be a matter of cash flow or cash management—there's just not enough money to put some aside for the future.

I talked earlier about "working smart," and I hope this book has helped you to do that. If so, you should be seeing improved cash flow and feeling you're in a better financial situation to put money aside for retirement. Now it's a matter of learning how to set your objectives, knowing what retirement plans are available, understanding the best way to supplement those retirement plans, and knowing how to deal with medical issues and retirement. In this last chapter, I'll show you how to "plan smart" so that you and your family can enjoy your retirement years in financial comfort.

*A good plan for retirement or semiretirement is one that makes your objectives as realizable as possible in light of the uncontrollable factors.*

## ◼Getting Started

How do you begin? There are many pieces to the puzzle: when to retire, medical issues, possible disability, family priorities, what you want your retirement to be like, and what you are willing to do now to make that possible. What is important is that you (and your spouse if you have one) define precisely what you want to occur at various points in your life and what steps you must take to make those things possible. The setting of objectives takes into account your desires for the future, but it is also subject to factors that you can't control. A good plan for retirement or semiretirement is one that makes your objectives as realizable as possible in light of the uncontrollable factors.

## ▄▄Defining Your Objectives

There are a number of factors to consider when planning for your retirement. These include the age at which you want to retire and your lifestyle during retirement.

### ■ Retirement age

Some contractors want to be finished working in their trades by a certain age. The ages I hear when I discuss this with contractors vary between as young as 55 and as old as "the last day of my life." Your objectives for retirement are very personal, so there is, of course, no one right age. Your Social Security benefits, your health, and family priorities will have a big effect on your choice. If you elect to take Social Security or other retirement benefits at an early date, each of those retirement benefits will be smaller than if you left them untouched until a later age.

**Q:** **What are the most important things to remember when planning for my retirement?**

**A:** Remember these six key rules:

1. Make your retirement plan a priority.
2. Start to plan now. Don't wait until retirement is forced on you by disability to begin your planning.
3. Consider how to organize your business to allow for a profitable sale at your retirement.
4. Use a qualified retirement plan to the maximum extent possible.
5. Do not underestimate your needs at the time of your retirement or overestimate the value of your assets.
6. Pay off your long-term debts before retirement.

**Age and health issues**  Plans for retirement and semiretirement also depend upon a number of factors you can't control. For example, if your physical ability to perform your trade is declining but you're not yet disabled in a substantial way, it may be tempting to set a planned date for retirement that is earlier than you would otherwise choose. Similarly, the health of other family members may have an impact on the timing of your retirement.

   If you do become disabled, you may be facing a forced retirement. Since disability is a constant threat to many contractors,

### ▄ TIP

**BE FLEXIBLE**
Because it's not always easy to know for sure when you'll be retiring, you need to make retirement plans that are flexible and allow for the best possible retirement at different ages.

**TIP**

**RETIRE DEBT-FREE**
Plan to have your mortgage, life insurance premiums, and any other long-term debt paid before retirement. This will make your retirement budgeting much easier.

retirement and disability can and do overlap. You should consider both situations together. At least some of the funds that you set aside for retirement should also be available at an earlier age if you need them for disability income.

**Family goals and retirement age**    If you have children and you have certain goals such as college that you want to see accomplished before you retire, this will also affect your retirement plans. If you are planning retirement or semiretirement within the range of ages that is customary, I strongly recommend that you plan to be free of a mortgage and other long-term debts by that time.

## ■ What does your retirement look like?

The next part of your planning can be fun. Use your imagination and paint a picture in your mind of what your retirement years will look like.

First, think about where you want to live. Do you want to stay put or move? If you plan to sell your home, talk with your accountant about the tax implications. Maybe you want to build the house of your dreams—the one that you never had the time to build because you were too busy building other people's houses. Will you want room for family and friends to visit? You'll need to run the numbers and consider taxes to see if you can afford to do that.

Think about how you want to spend your time once you're retired. For example, if you want to travel or maybe take up golf

---

**Painting Your Retirement Picture**

Your first step in retirement planning is defining your objectives. This is simply imagining what you want your life to look like in retirement. Here are some of the areas to consider:

- Your general standard of living
- Your type of residence (house, condominium, rental)
- Medical care
- Working or not
- Recreational interests
- Provisions for children, if any
- Transportation needs
- Travel desires

or photography, you'll need some money to enjoy these activities. What will your medical needs be and how will you pay for them? What are your plans for your estate? What do you want to pass on to your heirs?

What should result from your careful thinking about these matters is a rough but reasonable approximation of the standard of living you'll be comfortable maintaining during your retirement years.

## Estimating Your Future Expenses

That was the fun step, but now comes the hard one: putting a dollar value on your choices. You'll need to determine, as accurately as possible, how much things will cost and how much money you will have from your various retirement income sources. This involves making reasonable estimates of what things will cost in the future. Yes, this is a tough task but an important one.

One way to do this is to look at the annual percentage increases of various items for at least the past 10 years, then make the assumption that future increases in costs will be of similar sizes. A good place to start would be the Bureau of Labor Statistics Consumer Price Index. An annual percentage increase ranging from 6% to 10% is probably realistic.

Once you have estimated future costs as accurately as possible, add 20% to 25% of your total to the amount you establish as your objective for income during your retirement years. The uncertainty of your future needs along with longer life expectancies make it even more important that you allow some breathing room in your overall estimate of expected expenses during retirement.

## Retirement Income: Putting Together the Pieces

Once you've done a careful job defining your objectives for retirement and putting a price tag on those choices, you are ready to look at your sources of income—your retirement plan. This is a process of assembling a number of pieces so that the total income you realize from them is sufficient to meet your needs.

### Retirement Income: Counting the Possibilities

- Social Security income
- Income from qualified plans
- Income from sale of business or buy-sell agreement with partner
- Savings and investment income
- Income from other work
- Disability insurance income
- Severance benefits
- Inheritances
- Damage awards
- Annuities and whole life insurance policies

**Q: Do I have to retire at age 65?**

**A:** No. You don't have to retire at any specific age. The value of your retirement assets, including your Social Security, will vary depending upon when you retire, but this does not mean that you must retire at any fixed time.

## ■ Social Security

There is no way that any contractor or anyone else can rely solely upon the money he will receive from Social Security to take care of all of his retirement needs. Social Security is only a piece of the retirement planning puzzle. It's an important piece but only a piece nevertheless. If you understand how it works, you will be in a better position to make the most out of the benefits that are available. I'll touch on generalities here. Since the Social Security laws change, check with the SSA or your accountant about your particular situation.

**Qualifications** Workers become entitled to Social Security by earning credits. You earn credits based upon your earnings for each year (in 2000, one credit for each $780 in earnings), but you're only permitted to earn four credits per year. A contractor doing any reasonable amount of work will earn the maximum of four credits in each work year.

Most people need 40 credits to qualify for benefits. There are reductions in the required number of credits for some disabled people and some survivors of Social Security recipients, but these shouldn't play a part in your planning. For your purposes, you will need 40 credits, which you should be able to earn in a normal 10 years of work. Almost all contractors will work far longer than necessary to earn their 40 credits, and if for some reason you don't, you will need some help to understand your special situation.

**Age requirements** Aside from disability, your present target age for receiving full Social Security benefits is between ages 65 and 67, depending upon your year of birth and current Social Security laws. Regardless of your "full" retirement age, you may begin receiving Social Security benefits as early as age 62. If you do this, however, your benefits will be reduced. The percentage reduction may be as low as 7% and as high as a little more than 20%, depending upon

### In It for the Long Run

Shortly after electing to begin his Social Security payments at age 63, Ed, a retired plumber, was offered a great job as a salesperson in a plumbing-supply business. Ed really liked the job (good hours, close to home, no physical work), but he didn't like the fact about half of his Social Security income would be reduced by $1 for every $2 he earned. When he put that together with the increased taxes that he would pay, this "great job" wouldn't make him nearly the money that he hoped. But Ed wisely looked at the long-range picture, too.

Ed is only about 18 months away from 65, when his Social Security would no longer be reduced by his earned income. The job would be much more lucrative then and he did not want to pass up the opportunity for perfect work that might not be available in the future. It was worth taking a hit for a year and a half knowing that in the long run he would be ahead of the game. When you consider your retirement choices, long-run thinking is very important.

how many years before age 65 you choose to retire and what year in the future you will begin receiving benefits. The SSA will do these calculations for you.

**Benefits available**  The amount of Social Security you will receive at retirement is based upon a somewhat complicated formula that takes into account the number of years you have worked and your average earnings during those years. To find out what your anticipated Social Security benefits will be, you can either call your local Social Security office or visit the SSA's website (http://www.ssa.gov) and complete (or request) a form SA-7004. The SSA will then send you a statement of what your earnings are expected to be.

**Earnings limitations**  There are some earnings limitations placed upon people receiving Social Security. Although there is no earnings limitation for any person aged 65 or older, there is a penalty for Social Security recipients aged 62 to 64. In 2000, for every $2 earned above $10,080 each year, people in the 62- to 64-year-old age group lose $1 in Social Security benefits.

Social Security payments may be taxable depending upon your income. As of the time of this book's publication, your income is taxable if the total of one-half of your benefits and all your other income is more than $25,000 ($32,000 if you are married, filing jointly). The $25,000 limit also applies if you are married, filing separately, and lived with your spouse at any time during 2000.

If you are married and filing a joint return for 2000, you and your spouse must combine your incomes and your benefits to determine whether any of your combined benefits are taxable. Even if your spouse does not receive any Social Security benefits, you must add your spouse's income to yours to figure whether any of your benefits are taxable.

If you pursue employment after your Social Security benefits begin, you must take into account the possibility of having Social Security reduced if you earn more than the allowed income. One out of every two dollars is a big chunk of your earnings, but if the earnings are high enough, it may be worth reducing or losing your Social Security in order to receive them.

**Getting assistance with Social Security benefits**   Information about Social Security is available at Social Security offices all over the country, on the Internet (http://www.ssa.gov), and in brochures that are available in most bookstores. Most of the materials I have seen are written in fairly straightforward terms, but the rules and regulations and various factors that concern these benefits are so complicated that most people don't have the patience to figure out everything they want to know. This should be a matter that your accountant will help you with when you have questions or problems that you can't answer by yourself. In addition to help from your accountant, there are specialists in the field of Social Security benefits. If possible, I recommend that you avoid hiring specialists, most particularly lawyers. Social Security benefits are not typically large enough to justify paying extra costs to get them.

## ■ Qualified retirement plans

One of the most important decisions a contractor (or any other worker) can make involves the use of a qualified retirement plan. Qualified retirement plans are approved by the federal government through the IRS. You must use one of the approved forms of qualified retirement plans to receive the tax benefits of such a plan.

These plans, which receive very significant tax benefits under the Internal Revenue Code and state tax laws, are a no-risk way to increase your retirement funds. Because you can invest before-tax dollars, your money goes much further. It is well worth spending a little time to understand retirement plans.

The advantage of a qualified retirement plan is that the money deposited each year and the income earned on that money are not taxed until you draw it out—typically at retirement or disability and usually when you are in a much lower tax bracket. The result is simple: You can put away more money, and it will grow faster than it would using a nonqualified plan. Unfortunately, many contractors do not take advantage of these plans.

While the law makes these plans available to every employer and employee, some plans aren't realistic for typical contractors and can cost too much to establish and administer. It's important to select the correct plan for your use, unless you work for an employer who makes the choice. The first thing you must learn are the different types of plans. There are several forms of qualified retirement plans available, but some of them rarely if ever make sense for contractors.

**Individual Retirement Account (IRA)** Any individual with earned income may open an IRA and contribute up to $2,000 per year. If the individual or his spouse isn't a participant in an employer-sponsored, qualified retirement plan, the IRA contribution will be fully deductible. Otherwise, the IRA contribution may or may not be deductible depending upon the spouses' combined gross income.

In addition to conventional IRAs, you may have the option to use Roth IRAs. With the Roth plan, you pay the required taxes before you reach retirement age (with after-tax dollars). Thus, when you withdraw the funds, you do not need to pay taxes. There are some restrictions on the purchase of Roth IRAs dealing with your income level and the combination of other retirement plans.

Whether a Roth plan makes sense for you depends upon many factors, such as the length of time your plan exists, your age, your tax bracket at present, your likely tax bracket at the time you will be withdrawing moneys, and other factors. Discuss these options with

*One of the most important decisions a contractor can make involves the use of a qualified retirement plan.*

*The advantage of a qualified retirement plan is that the money deposited each year and the income earned on that money are not taxed until you draw it out.*

your accountant or financial advisor. In most cases, Roth plans are not advisable for contractors.

**Simplified Employer Pension (SEP)**  This plan permits the employer to contribute up to 15% of each eligible employee's compensation. Participants in this type of plan may also make contributions to an IRA.

**Simple plan**  With this plan, eligible employees may make salary deferral contributions up to $6,000. Employers must make contributions to each eligible participant.

**401(k) plan**  A 401(k) profit-sharing plan allows eligible employees to contribute a portion of their salaries before taxes to the plan. The maximum allowable contribution changes from year to year. For the year 2000, it is $10,500. The employer may match the employee contributions or contribute a different amount to each participant. In a typical 401(k) plan, the employer has a formula for matching employee contributions up to a certain amount.

The employer's payments on behalf of employees must meet a strict nondiscrimination test that prevents too much money from going only to the employees earning the highest incomes. If the plan does not satisfy the nondiscrimination test, it becomes "top-heavy" and subject to sanctions and corrections.

**Defined benefit plan**  This is a plan that rarely makes sense for any employer or employee, particularly for a contractor. In this plan, a fixed benefit at retirement is established for each eligible employee. This benefit may be as much as 100% of compensation to that employee but may not exceed $135,000 per year. The employer is required to make a contribution of a determined amount to the plan each year. The amount is determined by an actuary, and the calculations are quite complicated. Various events, such as the hiring of older employees who are close to retirement, changes in investment assumptions, and underfunding of these plans, cause very serious problems to occur.

**Money purchase pension plan**  In this plan, the employer is required to make an annual contribution of up to 25% of each eligible employee's compensation. No participant in this sort of plan may exceed an allocation of more than $30,000 in a single plan year.

### Qualified Retirement Plans: Making a Choice that Makes Sense

Discuss the various available retirement plan options with your accountant or financial advisor. When reviewing the plans, consider two primary issues to decide if a plan is suitable for your company: the plan's contribution requirements and the amount of administration needed. Because of these factors, the odds are high that two of the possible plans, the defined benefit plan and the money purchase pension plan, will not make sense for you. The 401(k) plan normally makes sense only for larger companies, rarely for small contractors. There may be a few circumstances in which a profit-sharing plan is sensible for small employers even though it requires more administration than other types of plans.

Generally, for contractors who work alone or in very small groups, simple plans, SEPs, and IRAs are the most likely choices. IRAs require almost no annual maintenance, and simple plans and SEPs require only a minimal amount.

**Profit-sharing plan**    In this plan, the employer makes a variable contribution of up to 15% of the total amount of compensation of eligible employees. A profit-sharing plan's contribution may be allocated to participants in several ways. It may be based upon compensation only, age at time of retirement, or a class-based formula. If a formula is used, it must be determined at the time the plan is established. As with money purchase pension plans, the maximum individual contribution is $30,000 per year.

**Employer contributions**    If you are self-employed or employed by a corporation or other form of business that has no other employees, you won't need to spend much time being concerned about eligible employees. But if you have employees, you must be aware that the benefits of plans that require employer contributions must be shared by all employees. The ways you are allowed to define eligibility and the relative amounts of money you must put aside for each eli-

**Q:** Once I have picked a retirement plan that works for me now, am I locked into it for life?

**A:** No. You can change from one qualified plan to another and can usually do it without a penalty. There may be some time restrictions. This is called a rollover.

gible employee are complicated. If you need to determine this, you will have to spend some time on it and should talk with your accountant or financial advisor.

**Getting help with qualified retirement plans** You will require some help to choose and establish the right form of retirement plan. If your accountant has knowledge in this area, she will be able to assist you. If not, there are special retirement fund advisors who can do this. If you choose to use one, bear in mind that consultants who help people establish retirement plans try to increase their business by administering them annually. In fact, the fee for establishing plans including all of the paperwork is often reduced provided that the client agrees to use the advisor for annual service purposes for at least a certain period of time. This is not what you want.

*You want an accountant who is capable of doing both your annual work for your corporation and your annual work for your retirement plan.*

Your goal is to select one of the forms of plans that requires relatively simple administration on an annual basis and to use your accountant for that purpose. You want an accountant who is capable of doing both your annual work for your corporation and your annual work for your retirement plan.

**Age considerations for withdrawals** There are limits to the retirement age at which you may start to receive benefits from plans. There are also possibilities for reducing those ages and for using retirement plans that have withdrawal provisions in the event of disability. These are very important matters to consider carefully when you establish your plan. You will definitely want your plan to provide as much flexibility as possible with regard to retirement age and withdrawal possibilities.

## ■ Value of your business

If you have made thoughtful decisions about the growth of your business, you will be in a good position when you choose to (or must) retire. In chapter 6, I mentioned ways to make decisions about the future of your business that take into account your future retirement. If you have one or more partners in your business at the time of your retirement and particularly if you have worked out a buy-sell agreement, you will be well on your way to using your interest in your business as a valuable piece of your retirement plan. Many buy-sell agreements provide for payouts over a number of years, which is a useful arrangement for the retiring partner as well as for the remaining partners.

If you don't have a partner or other plans for passing on your business, you might be able to sell your business to another contractor who is interested in purchasing your equipment and in having a ready-made clientele. I have seen such transactions work out for retiring contractors, although they are certainly not ideal because of the difficulty of finding an interested buyer and then putting a value on your business.

## ■ Savings and investments

Investing funds in retirement plans is not the subject of this book, but because savings and investments can and should be part of your retirement plan, I'll touch on a few highlights. There are today many ways to obtain good investment advice at virtually no cost. If you ask questions and look around, you'll find the investment information you need easily available. In fact, you will find a great deal of it in newspapers, on television programs, and on the Internet.

**Where to put your money**   You will need to make your investment decisions based on your own situation, but here are a few common tips:

- Look for a good combination of insured money market funds, highest-rating bonds (tax-frees are of no use in these plans since they are tax-exempt and pay lower interest), and well-chosen mutual funds for stocks.

- Put together a reasonable mix of investments that have high long-run security. No one who is planning to use these funds as a part of his retirement program should gamble with them.

- Bear in mind that most of the funds placed in such plans are going to be there for many years, even if unexpected withdrawals begin because of disability.

**Make savings and investments a priority**   If you're a typical contractor, saving and investing money is extremely difficult for you. The majority of contractors to whom I have spoken use an approach to savings that makes it virtually impossible. As difficult as putting money aside may be, it is necessary to have a certain amount of sav-

**TIP**

**RETIREMENT AND DISABILITY**
In planning for retirement, consider the possibility that disability or partial disability may affect your plans. Select a qualified retirement plan that allows you to withdraw funds if you become disabled.

ings, some portion of which is invested carefully and properly for retirement income.

While it is certainly true that such payments may somewhat reduce your lifestyle if they are substantial and you make them regularly, I can promise you that a reduced lifestyle while you are working is far better than reaching retirement years without a workable plan. You should view a sound and continuing program of savings and investments during your working years as an essential part of what you must do to make your entire life as happy and workable as possible. The best advice anyone can give you is to do it without fail.

*As you decide how much money you're going to place in your qualified retirement plan and how much in savings and investments, bear in mind that there is a significant tax advantage to the qualified plans.*

**Savings vs. qualified retirement plans**  If you're the only employee or one of very few employees working for your business and your personal financial success is essentially the same as the financial success of the business, then savings and investments come out of the same pocket as monies that are paid into your qualified plan. This would make it easy to conclude that if you make sufficient payments to your qualified plan, there is no need to make other payments to a retirement account for savings and investments. Theoretically, this is true, but it rarely works in practice. Very few contractors place enough money in their retirement plans to be able to give up one of the other financial pieces of a satisfactory retirement plan, which is savings and investments.

In addition, monies in qualified plans must be withdrawn in particular ways that are permitted by the laws that apply to them. Personal savings and investments may be spent at any time. They provide for the possibility of emergencies requiring a lot of funds at the same time and for big expenditures that would otherwise not be possible. For example, it might be less expensive in the long run for you to buy a small house, with no mortgage, at or near your retirement years. In light of your estate plans, buying might also make more sense than an alternative such as renting. Savings and investments allow for such possibilities. As you decide how much money you're going to place in your qualified retirement plan and how much in savings and investments, bear in mind that there is a significant tax advantage to the qualified plans. With the help of your accountant, who must fully understand your qualified plan, you should be able to make an intelligent choice regarding how to allocate these payments between a business that you control and your own personal funds.

**Savings and investment income projections** As with each piece of your retirement program, it's necessary to determine as accurately as possible how much income will be generated by the savings and investments you're working to establish. This isn't a simple thing to do, since you must estimate how much total value will be in your savings and investments at times in the future. Even if you assume that you won't fail to make the payment you establish every month, you must still take into account changes in interest rates and the uncertain possibilities regarding the growth of investment funds over a relatively long period of time.

---

### Don't Gamble with Your Retirement

Fred, a small general contractor in his late 50s, had planned carefully for his retirement. Among other assets, Fred had a joint investment account with his wife, which held more than $150,000 worth of mutual funds, high-quality bonds, and insured money market accounts.

After many years of doing residential and small commercial work, Fred submitted the winning bid on an addition to the local elementary school. Since this was a public job, Fred was required to have payment and performance bonding. Fred had no difficulty obtaining bonding from a reputable surety company, but it required that he and his wife provide a guaranty. The guaranty exposed all of the assets of Fred and his wife, including the investment account, to the bonding company if it was required to pay money to the public authority.

Unfortunately, Fred did not do well on the school job, and his construction company was not able to complete it. The surety company hired a takeover contractor to make good on its obligation and spent more than $250,000 finishing Fred's company's contract. Since the surety company had a guaranty from Fred and his wife, they had no problem taking the retirement investment account.

*Never—alone or with your spouse—sign any form of guaranty or pledge unless you are willing to lose the money.* The protection of a corporation is worthless once you give a personal guaranty or pledge. There is no job that is worth betting the ranch.

**Q:** **What kinds of work can I do in retirement?**

**A:** There are many opportunities that allow you to use your experience more than your muscles:

- Home-based businesses, particularly using the Internet or sales
- Consulting
- Estimating
- Supervising

Ask your accountant for help with this. Although all such advice will always depend upon uncertainties regarding future interest rates and investment results, accountants and others with sound financial experience know how to make realistic future estimates.

**Don't risk your retirement** My final advice regarding savings and investments for retirement is that you should never, under any circumstances, place such money at risk. While you are growing your business, you might find it tempting to use assets such as your home, your savings, or other retirement investments as collateral to guarantee a loan. Don't do it. Although laws provide a great deal of protection from creditors for qualified plans, there is no protection at all provided for personal funds.

Once you've accumulated savings and investments for retirement over a period of time, the loss of such retirement assets is not replaceable. There is no business opportunity that can justify taking a risk with this money.

## ■ Working during retirement

Chapter 10 covered various ways to work if you become disabled. You might also consider those possibilities if you need to supplement your retirement income. Not only will continuing to work on a limited basis provide you an additional income, but it also could help you in the area of medical benefits. Be sure to consider these factors and review them with the appropriate people before you make a decision regarding working during retirement. If you do work, remember that it may have an effect on your Social Security.

---

**Retirement Work and Medical Coverage**

Your choice about retirement work may affect the availability of the medical insurance you are using. For example, if you live in a state that guarantees every working person the right to purchase certain forms of medical insurance at prices that depend only upon certain factors, a choice to work during retirement, even at a very reduced level, may entitle you to medical insurance you could not otherwise obtain. This is a complicated matter that you should discuss with your medical insurance broker.

## ■ Other sources of retirement income

In addition to Social Security, qualified plans, savings and investments, and other work income, there are miscellaneous sources of income that you may use during your retirement. These might include, for example, disability insurance income, severance benefits from your employer for a limited period of time, inheritances in various forms including certain forms providing long-term income, damage awards in regard to negligence claims, and annuities that may have been acquired in numerous ways. Although each of these possibilities exists for only a limited group of retired contractors, there are a significant number of contractors who have had the good fortune to have one or more of them. You should check out every possibility that may provide you with retirement income to add to the income you receive from the more traditional sources.

## ■ Balancing Income with Expenses

The final step in determining whether your retirement income is sufficient to meet your objectives is to add together all of the pieces I have discussed. Do this carefully and realistically because it will be the basis for you to determine whether you have planned adequately or, if you have not, how far you have to go. Two things you should bear in mind as you add up your retirement income sources are the number of years for which you will receive income from each source and the availability of that income on a monthly basis.

*Two things you should bear in mind as you add up your retirement income sources are the number of years for which you will receive income from each source and the availability of that income on a monthly basis.*

## ■ Length of benefit payments

First, determine how long a period of time each source of income will pay you. Some sources, such as Social Security, will pay indefinitely. Other sources, however, involve making assumptions about how much interest you will earn and how long you will live. I'm not going into issues of life expectancies or fluctuating interest rates, but suffice it to say that you should work with an accountant or investment advisor to make sure that you understand how much of your investment will be available for you to use and how long that investment should last. It is critical that you don't use up your retirement funds prematurely.

### ■ Monthly calculations

Make all of your income calculations on a monthly basis. Most people are accustomed to receiving and paying their bills monthly, and this won't change during retirement. If you are using sources of income that don't make it possible for you to draw monthly income from them (such as most bonds and all long-term savings certificates), you need to smooth out your monthly retirement income so that you can pay your bills as they come due.

## Medical Care during Retirement

An important consideration for your retirement years is the availability of medical care for you and your family. There are two primary sources: Medicare and private Medicare supplement insurance.

### ■ Medicare

*It's not a good idea to rely solely on Medicare for medical coverage.*

The starting point for considering medical care during retirement years is Medicare, the national program to provide basic health insurance to people 65 or older and many (but not all) people with disabilities. Although a few people qualify for both, Medicare and Medicaid have nothing to do with one another. Medicaid is a health care program for low-income people with almost no assets. Unless you disregard everything in this book and have terribly bad luck as well, you will never be entitled to Medicaid.

There are two parts to Medicare. The hospital insurance part ("Part A") helps to pay for inpatient care and limited follow-up services. The medical insurance part ("Part B") helps to pay for doctors' services, outpatient hospital care, and other medical services. Most Americans receive Part A of Medicare when they reach age 65, unless they become disabled and receive it sooner.

Although you will most likely qualify for Part A of Medicare, Part B is not automatic. Unlike Part A, which was paid for by withdrawals from your income as you earned it, Part B of Medicare is optional for a monthly fee. Most people do choose Part B, which cost $45.50 per month in 2000.

The matter of Medicare, including the benefits and services it provides, how to enroll in it, and whether to use Part B, is somewhat complex. As with Social Security, you can find information in brochures that are available free at Social Security offices and for very little cost in bookstores. You can also look on the Internet. Seek advice in this matter if you need it, but avoid paying unnecessary money to lawyers and expensive consultants.

### ■ Medicare supplements

It's not a good idea to rely solely on Medicare for medical coverage. There are quite a few services you may need that are not covered by either Part A or Part B, and Medicare payments generally are too low to get the best services in any category. Many health care providers don't want to see Medicare patients, while others see them with great reluctance and even some hostility.

Look into purchasing a Medicare supplement insurance policy. Some of these policies are available through trade associations or general associations for older people such as AARP (American Association of Retired Persons). The premiums for such policies are generally reasonable and allow you to receive far better medical care than you would receive from Medicare alone. My advice is to include in your retirement planning the premiums for both Part B of Medicare and for a Medicare supplement insurance policy. Your independent agent or broker will have available a lot of information about such policies and will explain to you their advantages.

Unless you qualify for Medicare as a result of disability, you will not be able to take care of your medical insurance needs through Medicare and a Medicare supplement insurance policy until you reach age 65. As discussed earlier, you have a fair amount of work to do regarding medical insurance for you and your family for the rest of your lives.

*Unless you qualify for Medicare as a result of disability, you will not be able to take care of your medical insurance needs through Medicare and a Medicare supplement insurance policy until you reach age 65.*

## Retirement and Estate Planning

Estate planning is the process by which you determine who will get all of your assets after you die. It's not possible to say much about individual estate plans in a general book, but there are a few things that you should recognize about estate planning because they relate to the retirement matters that are discussed in this chapter.

- Think about what you would like to leave to your heirs and draw up a list of those items.

- See a competent lawyer and have her draw up a will. This is the only way that you can be sure that your heirs will get what you want them to get.

- Don't compromise your retirement so that you can leave a large estate.

Your lawyer may discuss with you variations of your retirement plans to allow your estate desires to be fulfilled as much as possible. Unless there is an unusually compelling reason, however, I recommend that you favor your retirement plans over your estate plans. You and your spouse, if you have one, will live with your estate plans for long portions of your lives.

The choices that I've covered here require making a number of decisions. These are decisions that have an impact on your lifestyle today and your lifestyle in the future. Having a sound retirement plan, even at the expense of a somewhat reduced lifestyle today and certainly at the expense of a large legacy, should be a high priority for you. The best reason for placing your retirement plans above your day-to-day desires is that if you're anything like the many contractors I have known, you have more than earned the right to some very good years at the end of your life.

If you and your wife have always dreamed of living in a little house on a beautiful lake and you can somehow work that out within your retirement plans, get that house and put this book on the porch to remind you that I recommended it! The steps I have recommended for planning retirement are intended to make it possible for you to live well after you have stopped working in your trade. Don't let other concerns, especially your estate, take your eye off that objective.

# Glossary

**Allowance**  The amount of money a contract provides for particular features of work or particular items. It is understood that owners pay for the cost of work or items in excess of allowances.

**Articles of incorporation**  The legal document used to form a corporation. This document is filed with a designated state office that grants corporations the status to operate a business. Articles of incorporation are sometimes known as the "charter."

**Billable hours**  The time a contractor spends performing his actual trade. This does not include time expended on chores necessary for the contractor to be able to do his work.

**Builder's risk insurance**  Insurance that protects additions being constructed on existing structures or new structures.

**Business expense**  An expenditure that is made for business purposes and is "necessary and reasonable."

**Buy-sell agreement**  An agreement between owners of a business that determines how voluntary and involuntary actions requiring the sale of an interest in the business will be handled. Buy-sell agreements establish the conditions under which sale to the business or the remaining partner will take place and the payment that will be made for the departing owner's interest.

**Capital expenditure**  A cost that may be deducted from gross income for tax purposes over a number of years in accordance with rules pertaining to depreciation.

**Catastrophic medical claim**  A very large medical claim related to an illness or injury that is ongoing, severely damaging, and very costly to address.

**"C" corporation**  A standard corporation in which the corporation pays taxes on its profits, and owners and other employees pay taxes on their salaries. Owners also pay taxes on any dividends they receive.

**Charter**  See **articles of incorporation.**

**Construction contract**  An agreement between a contractor and an owner or general contractor that provides that the contractor will do described work for an agreed price. Although written contracts are preferred, it is possible to make binding oral contracts.

**Construction management**  A system in which all subcontractors are employed by the owner and the construction manager manages the work for a fee.

**Damages**  The amount of money an injured person receives as a result of another person's negligence or breach of contract.

**Deductible**  The amount of liability that must occur before an insurance policy assumes responsibility for the damages or expenses. The insured party pays for damages or expenses up to the amount of the deductible.

**Deductible expense**  An expense that is deductible from taxable income. There are deductible business expenses and deductible personal expenses. See **business expense** and **personal expense.**

**Depreciation**   The manner in which the cost of a capital expenditure is deducted from your gross income for tax purposes over a number of years.

**Dividend**   Payments received by owners of corporations in proportion to the number of shares of stock they own. Dividends are rarely paid by contracting businesses.

**Employee**   A person who works for a particular business and receives his salary from it.

**Employer identification number**   A number provided by the IRS to a business that employs people.

**Enrolled agent**   A person who has been certified by the IRS as appropriate for the preparation of tax returns for others.

**Estate planning**   The process of planning for how you will dispose of your assets at the time of your death. Technically, your "estate" includes only those assets that are passable by will, but the term "estate planning" is used generally to include all of a person's assets.

**Estimate**   A contractor's best determination for an owner or general contractor of the price that will be charged for particular work.

**Estimated tax payment**   A payment that is required by the IRS or your state government in anticipation of a tax liability at the end of the year.

**Excess liability insurance**   Liability insurance that pays for damages to persons or property that exceed the amount that is covered by general liability insurance.

**Exclusion**   Features of work that are not included in a construction contract.

**Exclusionary period**   The period of time during which you must have a partial or total disability before payments under a disability insurance policy begin.

**FICA**   This term stands for Federal Insurance Contributions Act and includes Social Security and Medicare payments.

**Fixed cost**   A cost of doing business that does not depend upon particular jobs.

**401(k) plan**   A type of qualified retirement plan in which the employer matches some of the employee's contributions to the retirement plan. See **qualified retirement plan.**

**FUTA**   This term stands for Federal Unemployment Tax Act. These are federal unemployment taxes that the federal government requires certain businesses to pay.

**Gatekeeper physician**   A general physician to whom a person covered by a health maintenance organization is assigned. See **health maintenance organization**.

**General contractor**   A contractor who enters a contract with an owner that requires the provision of services of a number of trades. A general contractor obtains these trades by engaging subcontractors.

**General liability insurance**   Insurance that protects corporations and their owners from liabilities that arise when persons or property are damaged.

**General overhead expenses**   Expenses involved in running your business that are not related to particular jobs. See **fixed cost.**

**Good faith**   A sincere effort to accomplish the work required by a contract as precisely as possible.

**Gross profit**   The profit a business makes before certain expenses are deducted from it. The expenses that are deducted from gross profit may include such things as taxes, insurance, depreciation, and amortization.

**Guaranteed renewable insurance**   Insurance, particularly life and disability insurance, that guarantees you the right to renew the policy for a fixed number of years at established premiums.

**Health maintenance organization (HMO)**   A form of health care insurer that provides services to people through a network of medical service providers. People covered by this form of insurance are assigned to a general physician (gatekeeper) who determines what other medical services, tests, and drugs those people will receive.

**Home-office deduction**   A deductible expense allowed to someone who uses a home office that is exclusively used for business purposes.

**Hourly rate pricing**   Pricing of jobs that is based upon an hourly rate for you and every other worker. The hourly rate is a combination of the amount of money you want to earn for your services and the hourly cost of your general overhead.

**Impossibility**   An unexpected condition that makes precise performance of a contract impossible. The condition could be a natural condition such as a hurricane or a manmade condition such as unavailability of the items specified.

**Independent agent or broker**  A person who sells insurance and is not an employee of an insurance company or an agent for only one insurance company. Independent agents or brokers are free to sell you insurance from many companies and to make recommendations between the companies. Many are members of the National Association of Health Underwriters and various state associations.

**Independent contractor**  A person who is not employed by a business but does particular work for it. An independent contractor does not receive a salary and controls the manner in which he does his work.

**Individual retirement account (IRA)**  A simplified form of qualified retirement plan in which the employee is permitted to place up to $2,000 per year ($4,000 per year for husband and wife) into the plan. See **qualified retirement plan**.

**Letter of agreement**  A simple form of construction contract between a contractor and an owner or general contractor. This form of construction contract is typically prepared by the contractor.

**Liability**  Responsibility for harm that is caused by a business. Harm includes negligence, intentionally wrongful conduct, and breaches of contract. It also includes the actions of the employees of a business.

**Limit of liability**  The maximum amount that will be paid under an insurance policy for a single occurrence or for all occurrences.

**Limited liability company (LLC)**  A relatively new form of business in which owners receive liability protection, but the LLC passes all of its profits to the owners for tax purposes.

**Mechanic's lien**  A lien on real estate that is available to unpaid contractors and suppliers in accordance with very technical state laws. Such a lien interferes with an owner's use of his real estate.

**Net profit**  The money earned by a business after the payment of certain expenses. Expenses may include taxes, insurance, depreciation, and amortization.

**Operating agreement**  An agreement between co-owners of an LLC that establishes how the business will deal with matters such as control and compensation.

**Out-of-network health care provider**  A provider of health care that is not within the group of providers with which an insurance company has special arrangements. Insurance companies differ as to the use of out-of-network health care providers and the compensation the insurance company provides for their services.

**Own occupation disability insurance**  Disability insurance that pays you in the event you are unable to perform your own occupation. This form of disability insurance is almost never available today.

**Partial disability**  A disability that prevents you from doing some of your work. Your work includes all possible work unless you have an own occupation disability insurance policy. See **own occupation disability insurance.**

**Partner**  One of several people who own a business together. The term "partner" is used loosely to include co-owners of corporations and LLCs, as well as partnerships.

**Partnership agreement**  An agreement between partners (or, in the case of a corporation, co-owners) that establishes how the business will deal with various matters such as control and compensation.

**Payroll taxes**  Money withheld from employees' salaries and paid to federal and state governments as required.

**Period of contestability**  The period during which a company providing disability insurance may contest your application in an effort to deny coverage to you.

**Personal expense**  An expense made for personal purposes and not business purposes.

**Point-of-source medical insurance**  This is medical insurance that provides care to insured people at one or several fixed locations. Point-of-source medical insurers have various requirements when services not provided at such locations are needed.

**Preexisting illness or injury**  A medical condition that existed before you purchased insurance coverage. Sometimes insurers believe that conditions that lead to later illnesses or injuries make the later injuries or illnesses preexisting even though they arose after insurance coverage was obtained.

**Preferred provider medical insurance**  A type of medical insurance based upon agreements between the insurance company and various medical service providers. The agreements establish rates that the preferred providers may charge for various services, and the insurance company pays the bills of preferred providers at the agreed rates.

**Premium**   The annual, semiannual, quarterly, or monthly cost of a particular insurance policy.

**Qualified retirement plan**   A retirement plan that receives special tax benefits in accordance with federal laws. These plans are approved and supervised by the IRS.

**Quarterly tax returns**   Tax returns the IRS and some state taxing authorities require you to file four times a year. These are required when individuals have no tax withholding and have a record of taxable income in past years. These are also required of corporations with a record of past income.

**Quote**   A contractor's estimate of the price of particular work.

**Retail sales tax**   See **sales tax.**

**Safe harbor**   A method for paying taxes as the year goes along which will avoid interest and penalties when final tax returns for the year are filed.

**Sales tax**   Taxes that states sometimes impose on the sale of goods and the sale of services. Contractors are required to collect and pay over to the state these taxes in states where sales tax is imposed on services.

**"S" corporation**   A corporation in which the corporation's profits are passed to the owners and the corporation itself pays no taxes.

**Self-employment tax**   A tax that is imposed on individuals who work for themselves.

**Sole proprietorship**   A business that is owned and operated by an individual person. There is no formal business entity in sole proprietorships.

**Start-up expenses**   Expenses that are incurred when a business is started.

**Subcontractor**   A contractor who performs a particular trade for a general contractor or an owner.

**Subrogation**   The right of an insurance company to step into the insured party's shoes with regard to a claim. A waiver of subrogation provision in a construction contract prohibits a subrogation provision in insurance policies. Insurance companies may require additional premiums to permit a contractor to agree to such a provision.

**Substantial performance**   Accomplishment of the work required by a contract that is not technically perfect but meets the objectives of the contract.

**Surety company**   A company that provides a payment and/or performance bond with respect to a construction contract.

**Takeoff**   A contractor's determination of the work required of his particular trade by a set of general plans.

**Takeover contractor**   A contractor who finishes a job that was started by another contractor who is unable or unwilling to finish it.

**Tax filing deadline**   The date by which tax returns for the previous year need to be filed for individuals and corporations. This date is April 15 except in unusual instances in which a business is permitted to use a fiscal year that is different from the regular calendar year.

**Term life insurance**   Life insurance that covers you only for as long as you pay premiums.

**Total disability**   A disability that prevents you from doing any of your work. Your work includes all possible work unless you have an own occupation disability insurance policy. See **own occupation disability insurance.**

**Unemployment insurance**   Insurance required by states to compensate individuals for limited periods of time when they lose their jobs.

**Unrestricted reimbursement medical insurance**
This type of medical insurance pays for medical services received from third parties, subject to exclusions. This type of medical insurance rarely exists today.

**Variable cost**   A cost of doing business associated with a particular job or jobs.

**Workers' compensation insurance**   Insurance required by states to protect employees who may become ill or injured as a result of their work.

# Index